TRIMTAB PRINCIPLE
Trimtabs are small steering devices used on ships and airplanes used to demonstrate how relatively small amounts of leverage, energy, and resources strategically applied at the right time and place can produce maximum advantageous change.

Published by Applied Research and Design Publishing, an imprint of ORO Editions.
Gordon Goff: Publisher

www.appliedresearchanddesign.com
info@appliedresearchanddesign.com

USA, EUROPE, ASIA, MIDDLE EAST, SOUTH AMERICA

Graphic Design: Trevor M. L. Berreth
Text: Darla Lindberg and selected Case Study Contributors
Project Coordinator: Kirby Anderson

10 9 8 7 6 5 4 3 2 1 First Edition

Library of Congress data available upon request. World Rights: Available

ISBN: 978-1-939621-64-1

Color Separations and Printing: ORO Group Ltd.
Printed in China.

International Distribution: www.appliedresearchanddesign.com/distribution

ORO Editions makes a continuous effort to minimize the overall carbon footprint of its publications. As part of this goal, ORO Editions, in association with Global ReLeaf, arranges to plant trees to replace those used in the manufacturing of the paper produced for its books. Global ReLeaf is an international campaign run by American Forests, one of the world's oldest nonprofit conservation organizations. Global ReLeaf is American Forests' education and action program that helps individuals, organizations, agencies, and corporations improve the local and global environment by planting and caring for trees.

OUTSIDE THE SKIN:

SYSTEMS APPROACHES TO SOCIETY'S LARGER STRUCTURAL ISSUES

DARLA V. LINDBERG

TABLE OF CONTENTS

7   **ACKNOWLEDGEMENTS**

9   **PREFACE**

20   **INTRODUCTION**

Planting acorns we will never harvest
The elegance of complexity
The organization of phenomena
The non-reductive

29   **DOUBT**

The most underrated human gift
A culture of control
The Social Contract
The Shadow of the Future
Nature, the genome of diversity
Natural systems agriculture
Intelligence architectures

47   **INDETERMINACY**

Impossible to plot culture
The Skyscraper Theorem
General Systems Theory
Information Theory
Postmodern complexity
Generative and fanciful
An isomorphism
The canon and the fugue
The fringe to center
Poro[U.S. Border]s: the place of policy

117   **SYNCHRONICITY**

The greatest status revolution
Parallelism
Asymmetrical information
Perturbance
The twenty-year generational clock
Theory of cycles
Twenty-year lag and why it matters
Moralist turned economist
Early frost and finance
TEDxPSU 2015: What motivates influential people?
Follow the money
Groupthink

227   **PREPARING FOR THE HARVEST**

The implement

229   **BIOGRAPHIES AND CASE STUDIES**

U.S.-Mexico Border Wall; Dave Maple
Property: Resource or Right?; Sara Pettit
Mapping the Institutions: The Big Six, Deep-Rooted
Institutions; Adam Longenbach
The Adirondack Park; Rebecca Slocum
Sharing Economy; Reinhardt Swart
Sustainable Aquaculture; Karalyn Slocum
Hart Island Case Study; Lindsay Connelly
The Poverty Industry; Tena Pettit

272   **CONCLUSION**

274   **POSTSCRIPT**

277   **ENDNOTES**

289   **BIBLIOGRAPHIES**

"Something hit me very hard once, thinking about what one little man could do. Think of the Queen Mary—the whole ship goes by and then comes the rudder. And there's a tiny thing at the edge of the rudder called a trimtab.

"It's a miniature rudder. Just moving the little trimtab builds a low pressure that pulls the rudder around. Takes almost no effort at all. So I said that the little individual can be a trimtab. Society thinks it's going right by you, that it's left you altogether. But if you're doing dynamic things mentally, the fact is that you can just put your foot out like that and the whole big ship of state is going to go.

"So I said, call me Trimtab."

Buckminster Fuller (February 1972)

ACKNOWLEDGEMENTS

Just as a system is a part-to-the-whole in a time-space relationship, this work is truly the result of all the great people and minds I have met and worked with over the years. So, perhaps this book and its pages will be seen as a heartfelt "thank you" to everyone who inspired and, then, confirmed the relevance and urgency of this topic presented this way. Without a doubt, the people who deserve the most credit for my approach to systems thinking are my parents. They left an indelible mark on everyone who knew them. Hard-working, strong, gentle, funny, courageous, generous, loving and luminously lovely people, I have yet to witness anyone who lived with more tenderness and humility towards their land, their family, their animals and their seamless life. Yes, I studied and read and worked to build this material over the years, but it's their example and wisdom that originated this work. Then, learning to build my own seamless life came with the sheer joy and privilege of being a mom to my sons, Trevor and Teague and my stepson, Todd. Their patience and understanding, their humor and way of seeing the world amaze me, still. I love watching them become their own persons, grasping their own powerful presence to affect those around them the way they do. I also owe my family, friends and colleagues so much. Conversations over coffee, lunch, dinner, wine, studio reviews, road trips, trips down memory lane, our shared love of a "thesis" and of "work" and lively discussions of current events, politics, and you name it, are all echoed in this work. You will recognize yourselves in these pages. And my students—thank you. Your courageous grappling with this material to render solutions and insights to some of the world's most pressing problems gives me enormous hope. Your continual urging after each semester to "write that book." kept me motivated to present this material this way. Thank you, Trevor, for carefully and beautifully putting this all together in the end. I could never have done what you do so patiently and tirelessly. Particular thanks to the Case Study contributors. Their work illustrates how a design thesis is enriched and made relevant with research done this way. Limited by space, their work is exemplary of the, literally, hundreds of topics benefiting from a systems approach to understanding how the world works and the resultant innovative approaches to institutional design. Thank you, Trevor, for your adeptness to capture the work and writing so perfectly in the cover and divider pages design. Thank you, Teague, for your earnest ability to unpack so many of these topics with me. As sons, you've especially lived this material with me and why I consider you my most plugged-in colleagues. I also cherish the memory of making final drafts while spending time among the people and powerful landscape of northern Arizona—that rare sky, my many new friends in Flagstaff, and the special time with my sister and her family. And anyone working on a book project should be blessed to have, at least, three kittens laying all over you, your work, and keeping it all slow and sweet.

PREFACE

Until it becomes obsolete, the *Yellow Pages* is still an actual book of "yellow pages," unique to every city and town and still delivered to every doorstep. Some as thick as several inches and others the size of a small pamphlet, the Yellow Pages could be described as syntactical cities. "Let your fingers do the walking" might not take you down streets and alleyways, but the alphabet orders and forms the logic for accessing a city as a collection of services, products, and people.

Figure 1. The Yellow Pages

Now imagine the Institutional City. In the same way the *Yellow Pages* captures the coming and going of businesses and services and people, the Institutional City is a cataloguing of the evolution of conventions and social contracts accessing and assigning power described by its regulations, policies, laws and decision-making structures. Institutions are formal like voting on an Election Day tax referendum for a new school, or they are informal like the local conventions guiding what is acceptable to wear to Sunday Mass. How amenable those institutions are to rethinking and reforming hints at the protractible characteristics of power and influence in dynamic settings. And since power is never easily relinquished once attained, it seems necessary to theorize the complex feedbacks between the changing mindset of a society, the events that trigger change, and how we reflect those changes in our institutional and environmental fabric over time. The point being, when all these dynamics come together within a time and a place, a defining milieu shapes our perspective towards the world and one another, framing the kind of thinker, designer, citizen, parent, or leader we become.

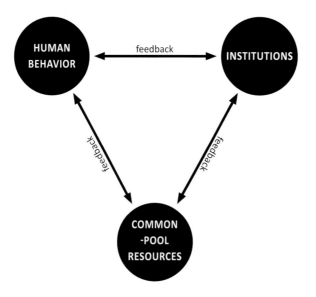

Figure 2. Fairness Framework

While this is not a book about politics or money or religion (the three topics discouraged at a family dinner), it is a book about the rational and irrational systems approaches involved in society's larger structural issues, granted politics, money, and religion play a prominent role. Topics in the various chapters such as Follow the Money, the Social Contract, and The Twenty-Year Lag alongside key theories such a General Systems Theory, Game Theory, Social Contract Theory, and the *Theory of Cycles*—with examples of Nobel Prize winning discoveries, i.e., Asymmetrical Information, the Lemon Law, Self-Organizing Societies—give us another way to think about the human condition. My own Fairness Framework is a model designed to illustrate the influential connections between Commons environments (environments we rely upon for our existence and our livelihood), the Institutions we create to manage those Commons, and our Human Behavior associated with maintaining the viability of both. Selected case study work by contributing authors illustrates an innovative application of five game theory games described in Elinor Ostrom's *Governing the Commons: the evolution of institutions for collective action* examining self-organizing societies.[1] Developed in a graduate seminar where her book was an important resource, the case studies look at Commons situations ranging from classic environments threatened by overuse and degradation to vulnerable new shared economies and technologies. A closer look at her games reveals a few aspects explored in the case studies: First, like it or not, there is an advantage to having sloppy institutions. Without an occasional gap or loop-hole in the system, the individual-entrepreneur nexus would be more difficult.

Second, a different view of the original "Cheat" in the Social Contract gets us closer to a grassroots opportunity to self-organize and rethink the rules for cooperation before things escalate to requiring outside or legal intervention. Solutions for collective cooperation that come from within a community are more likely to last longer than anything imposed from the outside or settled through litigation. And Third, there is no one-size fits all. Nested enterprises are essential to allow for local knowledge of unique complexity in a situation and, where necessary, to build in oversight at the state level and regulation at the national level. Considering an elephant's problem is staying cool in the summer and a bird's problem is staying warm in the winter, these group dynamics all have a scale for effectiveness. So does institutional design. There is no such thing as too little local involvement in some cases or too much governmental oversight in others. Knowing the difference is important. In a graduate seminar of 12-15 students, for instance, you have lively discussion and debate. Once that class balloons to 35 and beyond, the room grows quiet. The method of delivering the course material needs to accommodate those unique dynamics to insure a rich learning environment at either scale. We also need a collective view comprised of other expert knowledges, i.e., in conflict, resources, stability, governance, infrastructure, power, and the list goes on. Therefore, the political pitch that implores us to think there is "only one way" for everything is, frankly, irresponsible. It shows a lack of interest in effective leadership and biases power and greed over genuinely advancing the interests of the community. History's lessons are clear. Societies consisting of a one-party system, that lack diversity for checks and balances, or that don't safeguard the fair processes for participation in governance can become corrupt and unacceptable in most settings where some form of free or independent thinking is desired. Size matters and nesting these enterprises gives us the right input and the right feedback at the right time. One would think the most iridescent contribution of a Post-Industrial, Machine-Age, Advanced Technological, Free Society would be to understand the need and have the facility to build things that work well.

As a recent exercise, I mapped out what I call The Twenty-Year Lag. I used historic charts from the 1800s tracking crop production and major weather events, i.e., droughts and floods affecting crop yields. I used additional charts from the 1900s aligning those cycles with economic panics, recessions and market highs. I also used more recent mapping by asset management firms tracking stock market highs and lows, governmental leadership, unemployment and interest rates. Of course, events around the globe affect Wall Street, but the exercise triggered some new questions about influence. I then looked deeper and wider at the generational influence identified by the Strauss-

Howe Generational Theory (identifying generations by name, i.e., Baby Boomers, Gen Xers, Millennials, etc.) to understand the rootstock, the DNA, of a milieu. That gave me reason to look more carefully at each incremental twenty-year phase of human development, in particular, the phase of life when a generation is in a leadership position for policy formation and decision making. It shed light on the need to look less at the immediate generation in a position of leadership, and more at the mindset of a generation twenty and forty years before, and then, after us.

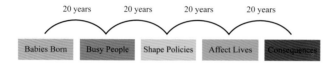

Figure 3. Twenty-Year Lag

To illustrate this, a recent study reported on National Public Radio presented Millennials' overwhelming preference for a socialist or communist society over their Baby Boomer parents' preference for a capitalist one. Researchers blamed this on a lack of knowledge of history. But not History-as-Survey-of-the-Past as the Baby Boomer generation construed it. Instead, History as current phenomenon chronicled in the fine grain complexity of intermingling systems of economics, environmentalism, policy formation, and power filtered through the dynamic lens of social media. So, while leaving home or learning from mistakes are considered rites of passage, even character building journeys to adulthood, the profound effects of these shifting generational world-view cycles on the physical wellbeing and economic resilience of the world remained under investigated. My mapping of, what I call, "The Twenty-Year Lag" sheds light on the importance of a new kind of history to account for "generational clocks."

A macro-to-micro whole systems analysis of political, environmental, and economic influences makes perturbations such as the Enron Scandal of 2001 possible. Possibly overshadowed by the 9/11 attacks on the World Trade Center that same year, but Enron is still considered the largest willful corporate scandal of the century. Self-interest and hubris destroyed economies, ecologies, retirements, and lives. Looking back, Reaganomics and deregulation were logical, even predictable, outcomes of a conservative generational pendulum swing. And then, twenty-years after its prime, Jeff Skilling, CEO of Enron Corporation at the time of its fall, is released from prison. And just at a time when conservative views are calling, again, for the deregulation of banks and the erosion of watchful environmental policy. The policy work done to safeguard us against incidents like

Enron are viewed as excessive and unnecessary. Edmund Burke worried about "those who don't know history are doomed to repeat it."[2] Those who can't identify the complexity circumstances distinguishing fraudulent arbitrage opportunities from naive coincidence are just plain doomed. Perhaps it's time to develop tools to better understand systems cycles and influences to safeguard us against the larger structural issues brought on by generational swings of institutional memory loss. In doing so, we develop skills, better for reading the world around us, enhanced with leveraged technologies and machine learning, contributing to a whole systems design imperative. To this end, representatives from every domain may accept the call to contribute to an institutional systems model of history to keep ready the hard work done to advance the projects of societal and environmental equity and justice.

Darla V. Lindberg

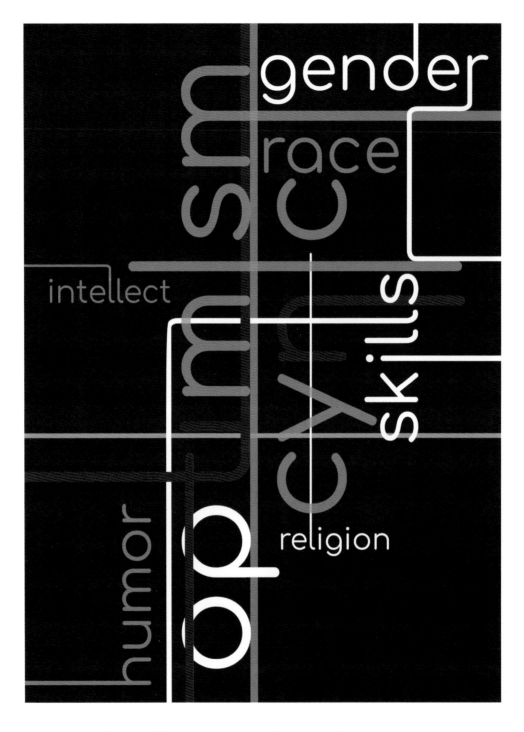

Figure 4. Illustration by Trevor M. L. Berreth representing institutional influencers depicted as an underground subway, communication and infrastructural system map.

So, why is the ability to extract a theory from a milieu useful? And how does a multi-layered understanding about our circumstance inform design? When unique domain knowledge, such as architecture, is part of the larger conversation of its time, the work brings together the events and moods making theory a relevant story to experience. I was fortunate to be able to witness a group of architects in Los Angeles do exactly this as they unpacked the impact of the L.A. Riots of the early 1990s.

Los Angeles in the early 1990s was a burgeoning metropolis. Boasting of its diversity, it represented a world-class city poised to be the gateway to the Pacific for the United States. Home to over 100 different ethnicities from all over the world, Los Angeles was perceived to be the international city that would lead America into the 21st century. The city had an African American mayor—Tom Bradley—elected with a rainbow coalition, meaning it included black, white, brown, and other ethnic minorities. Mayor Bradley and his rainbow coalition promised Los Angeles economic prosperity and hope for everyone. However, for a city which had not seen an economic downturn in over 50 years, L.A. discovered it was not immune from the 1990-91 recession which jolted the rest of America with the largest number of bankruptcies in the country's history. Then, the acquittal of the officers charged in the Rodney King beating on April 29, 1992 triggered the largest urban race riots in the history of the United States. In the process, it exposed the racial tensions simmering below the surface that led to violence towards victims being targeted on the basis of race.[3] Post-riots research unveiled some chilling facts. First, for a city affectionately known as "La La Land," the city learned it was suffering from the type and frequency of crime found in more mature cities around the world but with a significantly understaffed police force when compared to cities such as New York or Berlin.[4] Second, and perhaps more significant, the raw rage and hatred stemmed by racial tension was caught in real time on video and watched by millions streaming over the Internet.[5] For anyone born since 1992, this is their reality. Raw footage of news and events is captured on video by anyone. It wasn't the lead Los Angeles could have anticipated. But L.A. owned it—a defining moment that would forever change the world.

Darla V. Lindberg

*Figure 4. Los Angeles Riots; Headlines of
the Rodney King Beatings*

I attended a conference in Los Angeles a few years after the L.A. riots and witnessed several key thinkers of Architecture in Los Angeles—Eric Owen Moss, Frank Israel, Thom Mayne, Michael Rotondi—grapple with the challenge of extracting a theory from conditions of circumstance riveting for L.A, the country, and that time. In a town where history was Yesterday-Afternoon they aptly identified with the European tradition beginning with the Medieval and culminating instantly with the Baroque. They created singularly lush and idiosyncratic perfection and as fleetingly significant as where Madonna was last seen having lunch. Detailing was one-off and called up the craft and perfection one only sees in a celebrity's ageless face. Architects operated inside insignificant warehouses making overnight sensations and one-hit-wonders of a common build-to-suit office suite. Their courage reinforced my thinking about the power of architecture to capture the mood of a milieu. The riots were a landmark moment defining, in particular, the privatization of public space after 1992. L.A. architect and 1993 AIA/LA president, Kate Diamond was commissioned to design the air-traffic control tower for LAX shortly after the riots. Her office took lead on the rethinking of public space, including the elimination of public toilets. Universally, park benches became a topic for design competitions directed towards architecture students around the country. Now with armrests becoming the new normal, getting too comfortable or staying too long was discouraged in any public space. Therefore, Theory shouldn't be remote and taught the same as history without the whole systems narratives inducing it. Examples like this drive home that theory needs to be understood in the present as a tool for designers, and possibly more critically, for the general public. The L.A. architects' ability to look inside and outside of their own locally original disciplinary skin, to participate significantly in the shaping of an understanding of their larger societal structural issues, brought home this urgency for a designer's thoughtful facility with reading conditions of circumstance. That reading must have a lived understanding of history as a threading together of politics, institutional disruptions, money, fame, power, hubris, and justice in order to inform truly relevant design for a place and time.

Therefore, I began developing material for a course to unpack what had happened. Perhaps it was because my second son was born in 1992 at the height of the community outrage from the officers' acquittal on trial for the Rodney King beating. I needed a way for Theory to be current. In the process, I developed a model for nonlinear thinking which I will share later in the book. It asks architecture to be a wise seer of the political will, economics, labor, resources, power and place, not a naive fee-for-service fool enabling the work of injustice and incompetence. Material from that course grew over the years and would become this book. Inspired by thinkers and designers who felt their topic was important enough to make it accessible to a broad audience of intelligent and interested people, the course attracted students and faculty from every domain. I have always approached architecture as a framework for constructing knowledge about the world around us. So, the examples characterizing "architectures" of complexity important to understanding this approach are derived from overlapping the arts, the sciences, and the humanities and welcomes readers from any domain and background. The important thesis, then, is that architecture is a statement of a deep understanding of the interconnectedness between human existence, institutional influence, and vulnerable shared resources. They tell a story of *collected* wisdom.

This is hardly new. Prior to medical germ theory of the 1870s, architects like Marcus "Vitruvius" Pollio, a Roman architect and engineer in the first century B.C., had to have a collective understanding of disease, geography, climate, and biology in order to avoid placing a building among bad miasmas (bad air).[6] The renaissance man (lowercase), someone with profound knowledge and proficiency in a wide range of fields, is even more essential now. Yet, the key hazard of disciplinary thinking as we've evolved and refined it through academia, is to stop recognizing the power of the general public to influence policy and decision-makers. Soliciting a readership that does not isolate a work to any single domain or enterprise (like research or teaching) is essential to educating the future citizen.

Thinking about complexity (expert details) and thinking about systems approaches (broad brush) are useful tools as any philosophy would be. But, like all expert domain knowledge, discoveries become shrouded in jargon and technical terms intended for specialists. While these expert terms and concepts comprise essential insights to advancing and testing the unique physics or functions of systems, and research shows jargon actually doesn't get in the way of readers parsing the key points, placing these discoveries and breakthroughs only in scholarly journals deters the wider readership. Therefore, I argue here that these important ideas are worthy of disseminating to the intelligent general reader. Therefore, more technical explanations of thinking about complexity and thinking about systems approaches are replaced with illustrative examples, summaries of documentaries, and case studies intended not only to represent insights and discoveries but also to provide innovative translations for their application to real world problems. In addition, I celebrate my own productive lifetime grounded first growing up in natural systems agricultural practices and principles and then later working across and within multiple disciplines. Therefore, the shared language of the successful scenario naturally removes most of the jargon.

An architectural thesis should provide its audience an appreci-
ation for the situation that induced its giving, as much as, the
collective intentions of its architecture.

Therefore, a "project" in architecture is potentially a situation
or premise where there is a secure basis in terms of form or
content or intent.

Likewise, a "problem" is a unique reading of the entire situation and the isolation of the issues critical to an appropriate
and significant determining.

Finally, a "proposal" is an attempt at articulating a problem
architecturally. The "thesis" will be a statement comprehend-
ed through the inherited and debated language and craft of
architecture.

. . . . . .

Darla V. Lindberg

. . . . . .

INTRODUCTION

Let me begin with a retelling of the story of the oak beams in the Commons Room at New College, Oxford University built in 1386. The beams were replaced at the end of the 19th century. When it was time to replace the beams the Oxford forester informed the builders that the man who built the original ceiling back in the 14th century also planted the trees to replace them. They stood on Oxford University land, waiting to be cut down for just that purpose. Some say the story isn't true; others say it ought to be. The story serves to remind people *to plant acorns knowing they will never live to harvest the oaks*.

The story also illustrates the significance of exploring the part-to-the-whole in a space-time relation. Whether we are considering the relationship of the biology of the tree to its environmental ecosystem or the seasonal cycles and their effect on the migration of birds and disease spread, systems have rational and observable behaviors grouped here as synchronicity, indeterminacy and doubt. Briefly, where synchronicity captures how systems behave and interact with their environments, indeterminacy places systems in continual evolution and adaptation, leaving doubt with the notion that systems are never quite fully known. Based on theoretical work done in the mid 20th century on indeterminate systems, thinking in complexity is a stage of optimization in systems thinking. Complexity is to systems as the micro-is-to-the-macro. It's never a case of either-or, or complexity versus systems. Rather Complexity Thinking is a stage of behavior in a System's life-cycle. For example, we can imagine the story of the oak beams at the complexity level of the characteristics of an oak tree lending to its use in structure, and the university committees and designers and builders, even the daily mechanics of building. We can also value the larger systems lessons of social-environmental responsibility in making decisions today that will provide for another generation tomorrow. The dance is the same in anything.

Both complexity and systems thinking can be traced to earlier work on Information Theory and General Systems Theory and more recent works on complexity concepts. Systems theory is the study of the organization of phenomena and these ideas were attempts to present in a rigorous way the treatment of systems as a transdisciplinary science, meaning disciplines are transformed by their association with another domain knowledge. Their developments are particularly relevant to complexity thinking because they anticipated advances in information aggregation from multiple sources, not just advances in technology. Building on examples from across the arts, the sciences, the humanities and embracing technologies, my thesis on systems thinking deliberately interrogates disciplinary boundaries as a disservice to real knowing. In fact, as Architecture is a rich cultural story, I place it firmly in the middle of this critique. And we must not avoid the messy topics of politics, beliefs, and money because these are the seams of complexity details where communities and countries differ and divide.

Some foundational background knowledge about key contributors is worth establishing before we launch into the tool and model part of this material. Thinking about Complexity can be traced to earlier work in Cybernetics and Information Theory (communication, reception and feedbacks) and was supported by early advances at the time in computation.[7] Since thinking in complexity is an essential framework for comprehending the capacity of huge numbers of unique phenomena acting in synergetic relation, computation was the right technology at the right time. Characteristics of Complexity, then, explain the non-linear, indeterminate and irreducible complex systems linking till agriculture to urban infrastructure to global disease dynamics. An accountant is a Complexity thinker. They are no strangers to exactitude. *The elegance of complexity* is, you don't round off.

General Systems Theory (GST), on the other hand, is the study of the *organization of phenomena* in relation.[8] These are the big picture people. But what is important is not that a relation exists but that the structural similarities of expression, metabolism, and interaction inherent to a system, are not lost in the transformation resulting from a relation. Just as two musical notes will produce harmony or discord depending on their own properties, their strategic harmonic combination is the result of the design or composition of the integration in a way that respects full well the notes as systems operating uniquely intact. Composers don't expect these notes to warp or bend. Any dissonance is deliberate and their resolve back to harmony is designed. Likewise, GST seeks to explain the physics of how all systems work together in real life. Key phrases about systems thinking are "water seeks its own level" or "gravity prevails." An irrational human view of a rational system is rational. The locus of rich questions, then, resides in the context, the relation, the seam, the border, the dynamics and impacts where all systems collide. I do this both to interrogate "disciplines" (distinct from expertise) from doing a disservice when addressing how the world operates, and also to allow for approaches to design thinking that significantly resist the urge for generalizations when collaborating with other critical fields. For example, as one of my own research examples will illustrate later in the book, cities and sprawling incorporated or unincorporated settlements around the world are emblematic of some of the most complex institutional and socio-political systems at work today. Complexity characterizes efforts at the grassroots, the sovereign identity of these unique ecosystems and places; GST puts them in relation to other systems (global politics, finance and health). So, together, without seeking to replace traditional modes of inquiry, the work invites new skills, methods and models of design inquiry within the milieu. Outcomes serve to provide a more fluid collaborative process between policy making and researcher in which the traditional instruments of representation, inquiry, and collective action are transformed. Incorporating whole systems dynamics thinking to some of the world's most pressing problems has us look at local and global economies, ecologies, and communities to see cycles repeat and patterns evolve. And rather than limiting the work to one theoretical domain, the work unites mathematics, psychology, biology, game theory, and social network analysis. In that way, the work remains true to a central driving tenet of systems theory, in that each and every discipline has a role to play in solving many of humanity's most pressing problems, and that no one discipline can do it alone.

Aimed at solving complex problems, my approach to architectural research and design (broadly understood), then, intentionally embraces what Buckminster Fuller referred to as "comprehensive anticipatory design science."[9] Fuller combined an emphasis on individual initiative and integrity with whole systems thinking, scientific rigor, and faithful reliance on nature's underlying principles. While Buckminster Fuller is best known for his geodesic dome, the Dymaxion house, car, map, and the global electric grid, his overarching challenge was to redesign interrelated systems with the sole intention "to make the world work for all."[10] To accept this challenge is to deliberately work with other disciplines (not just sister disciplines) to explore, discover, invent, and even pioneer strategies for understanding and implementing complex solutions. Therefore, it is essential that architecture, and every domain, be part of an integrated strategy dealing with key social, behavioral, economic, environmental, policy, and geopolitical systems. Beginning with Buckminster Fuller in my opening few pages of the book makes sense. He considered himself a trimtab (his epitaph says "Call Me Trimtab").[11] Trimtabs are small steering devices used on ships and airplanes that demonstrate how relatively small amounts of leverage, energy, and resources strategically applied at the right time and place can produce maximum advantageous change. My contribution is to call attention to the complexity details involved in the seemingly innocuous choice—a single vote to tip the scales of leadership for a century. Or the connection between an event, a movement and a child's dream. At risk in this game is the effect of our human interactions on our finite Commons environments and the quality of the Institutions we create around those Commons. This requires a rich involvement of disciplinary knowledge and methods of knowing. Identifying factors and interactions that increase the robustness or weaken the resiliency of any unique community, environment, or shared commons as an essential ecosystem calls for a larger relational systems picture and a specificity—the complexity of a situation to actualize its potential—*the trimtab principle*.

"Systems" gets a mixed reaction. It's understandable. At best, systems reference a range of scholarly work in virtually every domain. Yet, everyone largely agrees it represents three universals: *Systems Theory* is the interdisciplinary study of systems; a system is an entity with interrelated and interdependent parts defined by its boundaries and is more than the sum of its parts, but rather the parts-to-the-whole; and changing one part of the system affects other parts and the whole system is adjusted with its environment. Beyond that, depending on the purpose or work function, the rich characterizations of systems from the theoretical to the practical support one another significantly and without conflict. The goal of Systems Theory is simple: to systematically discover a system's dynamics, constraints, conditions, and elucidating principles (purpose, measure, methods, tools, etc.). Correlatively, the goal of *applied* systems is to discern the levels of nesting within every field for achieving optimized equifinality.

General Systems Theory is about the broader concepts and operations of how things work together, as opposed to particulars of any unique domain. Dynamic and active systems are different from more stable or passive ones. Where active systems interact in characteristics and approaches, passive systems are the elements or structures being processed. The term "general systems theory" originates from Ludwig von Bertalanffy's general systems theory.[12] Others shared his interests. Kenneth E. Boulding was interested in broader relationships of the empirical world and worked to develop more systematic theoretical constructs to observe that world.[13] William Ross Ashby's pioneering work in Cybernetics focused on communication and feedbacks more currently known as machine learning.[14] Anatol Rapoport worked in mathematics, psychology, biology, game theory, and social network analysis. Anyone studying Architecture most likely read Anatol Rapoport in their first year of undergraduate education. If you read his work more completely, you would naturally be interested in social interaction and network analysis and the mathematical tools involved in conflict, cooperation and contagion. Similarly, Walter Gropius, teaching at Harvard, was instrumental in establishing the reputation of the Bauhaus in the United States. He asserted, "our guiding principle is that design is neither an intellectual nor a material affair, but simply an integral part of the stuff of life, necessary for everyone in a civilized society."[15] My own undergraduate thesis advisor, Cecil Elliott, studied under Gropius at Harvard, and presented in his own work the interconnectedness of small tools and inventions to a larger cultural story.[16]

Sociological systems thinking started earlier, in the 19th century. Stichweh states, "...since its beginnings the social sciences were an important part of the establishment of systems theory."[17] The two most influential suggestions were the comprehensive sociological versions of systems theory which were proposed by Talcott Parsons since the 1950s[18] and by Niklas Luhmann since the 1970s.[19] References include Parsons' action theory and Luhmann's social systems theory.

The diverse growth of Systems Theory can be exemplified by the range of key contributors including the work of biologist Ludwig von Bertalanffy,[20] linguist Bela H. Banathy,[21] sociologist Talcott Parsons,[22] ecological systems with Howard T. Odum,[23] Eugene Odum,[24] and Fritjof Capra,[25] organization theory and management with individuals such as Peter Senge,[26] interdisciplinary study with areas like Human Resource Development from the work of Richard A. Swanson,[27] and insights from educators such as Debora Hammond and Alfonso Montuori.[28] As a transdisciplinary, interdisciplinary and multiperspectival domain, the area brings together principles and concepts from ontology, philosophy of science, physics, computer science, biology, engineering, geography, as well as, sociology, political science, psychotherapy—as in family systems therapy—and economics, among others. Systems Theory thus serves as a bridge for interdisciplinary dialogue between autonomous areas of study as well as within the area of systems science itself. In this respect, one can imagine the possibility of misinterpretations. Therefore, von Bertalanffy believed a general theory of systems was an important regulator in science to guard against superficial analogies that are both useless and harmful to science and its application. Others remain closer to the direct systems concepts developed by the original theorists. For example, Ilya Prigogine, of the Center for Complex Quantum Systems at the University of Texas, Austin, has studied emergent properties, suggesting that they offer analogues for living systems.[29] The theories of autopoiesis of Francisco Varela and Humberto Maturana represent further developments in this field.[30] Important names in contemporary systems science include Russell Ackoff,[31] Ruzena Bajcsy,[32] Bela H. Banathy ,[33] Anthony Stafford Beer,[34] Peter Checkland,[35] Barbara Grosz,[36] Robert L. Flood,[37] Allenna Leonard,[38] Radhika Nagpal,[39] Fritjof Capra,40 Warren McCulloch,41 Kathleen Carley,42 Michael C. Jackson,[43] Katia Sycara,[44] and Edgar Morin,[45] among others.

A concern among the widespread use of Systems Theory is the loss of translation when "theory" or "science" are being considered in different contexts. By becoming such a widespread way of thinking of the interdependence of relationships between entities, Systems Theory became a very general term. A system in this frame of reference can contain regularly interacting or interrelating components, cells, or groups. This relationship between components and their environments can be seen as the foremost source of complexity and interdependence within a system. In most cases, one cannot know the whole from analysis of the parts in isolation. Bela H. Banathy is among the founders of a systems society and has made major contributions to systems theory believing the purpose of science was to benefit humankind.[46] For the Primer Group at ISSS, Banathy shared his view:

> The systems view is a world-view that is based on the discipline of systems inquiry. Central to systems inquiry is the concept of System. In the most general sense, system means a configuration of parts connected and joined together by a web of relationships. The Primer Group defines system as a family of relationships among the members acting as a whole. Von Bertalanffy defined system as elements in standing relationship.[47]

We find similar ideas in learning theory developed from the same fundamental concepts where key understanding results from knowing concepts both in complexity and as a larger whole. In fact, Bertalanffy's organismic psychology was consistent with the learning theory of Jean Piaget.[48] Some consider interdisciplinary perspectives an essential part of breaking away from post-industrial models of thinking, wherein subject matter is kept in tidy domain boxes—history is history and math is math and art and science are specializations and teaching is behaviorist training. Peter Senge, in particular critiqued modern educational systems as fragmenting knowledge and hampering holistic learning which became a model for school separate from life and encouraged a machine-age way of thinking.[49] In this way, some systems theorists such as Max Weber[50] and Emile Durkeim[51] attempted to develop alternatives to orthodox theories which have grounds in classical assumptions. Similar contributions were made by Frederick Winslow Taylor[52] in scientific management. The work of all these theorists sought holistic methods of developing systems concepts that could integrate with different areas. Not to do away with expert knowledge in any one domain but to enable the non-reductive and enrich a larger knowing and greater specialist breakthroughs.

DOUBT

DOUBT

The most underrated human gift

Possibly the most underrated gift humans are endowed with is doubt. Doubt teaches us that all basic and fundamental processes cannot be thought of in a reductive way. In fact, all biological and social applications have proven to be irreducible, co-evolutionary and stochastic. The Human Genome Project (HGP), for instance, ushered in a new way of comprehending how huge numbers of phenomena can be processed with complete elegance.[53] Downloaded, the HGP consists of a long string of Ts, As, Cs, and Gs. The genius of the HGP wasn't that it presented the genomic code of using a little bit of information (in genes) to achieve enormous complexity (Homo Sapiens) but more significantly demonstrated how *useful* information could not be reductive.

Doubt is simultaneously quieted and amplified with technology. Searching the Internet for symptoms, causes, and treatments of any disease or machine malfunction is evidence of that. Showcasing technology at its best and its worst, the Internet is possibly the greatest status equalizer in our time. Everyone has immediate access to everything. Therefore, Doubt is celebrated through interdisciplinarity—decision fusion linked to disease spread to economic health. Having immediate access to domain knowledge facilitates a philosophy converging new insights, methodologies, and discoveries and transforms disciplinary knowledge. In doing so, transdisciplinarity essentially provides the blueprints for constructing new gene, bio, and intelligence knowledge systems. As Rachel Carson's work poignantly portrays, intellectual tools this fluid are necessary for understanding how a single decision moment along-side centuries of other decision moments can alter life on the planet. In this way, resilient systems are revered as adaptable to conditions and contexts while they remain recoverable to an original idea, theme or harmonic structure. So, drawing attention to the shadow, and not the thing, Peter Berger writes, "When we look at revolutions, we find that the outward acts against the old order are invariably preceded by the disintegration of inward allegiances and loyalties. The images of kings topple before their thrones do."[54] Doubt is the system behavior that drives us forward or turns us back in hesitation. Either way, doubt is at the foundation of *a culture of control.*

It would be naïve to think life could be fair. As the saying goes, "a sucker is born every minute." Even at the cellular level, life is motivated by self-preservation. The Public Goods Game, part of game theory, illustrates the social interactions of cancer cells which, as "free-riders," consume common resources without paying the production costs to support health. Joseph W. Meeker in his book, The *The Comedy of Survival: Literary*

Ecology and a Play Ethic describes how a mother bear might encourage her cubs to play as a coercive way to teach survival techniques essential for the wild.[55]

In Rousseau's characterization of the Stag Hunt, Doubt is channeled to positive gains by building in assurances for co-operation. Also known as an "assurance game," or "coordina-tion game," even the "trust dilemma," the Stag Hunt gives us insight into the problem of social cooperation, where trusting large groups of strangers is necessary to accomplish larger gains. In the Stag Hunt, hunters have two options. They can either hunt hare or hunt stag. Hunting stag is not easy, but the payoff is great. To "bag the buck" requires the cooper-ation and coordination of many. Hunting hare, on the other hand, is easy. But the payoff is small. More significantly, be-cause societies champion risk taking, those off hare hunting alone while the many are hunting stag will be labeled a Social Sucker, a Fool. "It's my choice," you might say, to live slower, smaller, on less. That is commendable, and even desirable at many levels. Don't get me wrong. But we're talking about the Rational. The more you leave on the table, the more there is for others to take. The more you contribute to the welfare of the needy, means others get to ignore them. Knowing the difference means you recognize the political decisions of the Haves to reduce welfare support for the Have Nots. In the rational world, something's gotta give.

Formally, the Stag Hunt is a game with two pure strategies, one that is risk dominant—you hunt stag with the group for the larger payoff, or one that is risk averse—you hunt hare alone and settle for the lesser outcome.[56] In either case, Trust is a function of hunting like the group. Triggers are an essential tool in the Stag Hunt game used to alter the status quo. If Doubt ushers in, cooperation breaks down in the group, or factions decide to splinter off and hunt hare, a strategic decision to switch and hunt stag can excite the group into working through their doubt and cooperate for the greater outcome. Likewise, if the status quo has been risk dominant pressuring the group to take greater and greater chances, a "free-rider" can drop back and benefit from the efforts of the group without engaging in the risks of the hunt. Trust is a paradox—it can arise sponta-neously by strategically interacting individuals. Doubting, on the other hand, may also simultaneously take over when mem-bers of a group decide it's time to walk away. And it can be nurtured because of a presupposed account of agent rational-ity—doubt in the ability to sustain interest points to a logical end. The classic Run-on-the-Bank is the outcome when a group of people withdraw their money from the bank, collapsing the system out of collective fear.

The Stag Hunt works in society because the Fool is the doubter, the un-trusting one on the other side of the Trigger. Therefore, as played out in the Stag Hunt game, the level of Trust in any relationship is directly proportional to the level of risk and gain to be made over time. The Stag Hunt has been used to characterize any endeavor that requires cooperation of many to achieve arbitrage results. Considering the compounding of participation needed to make Wall Street, Main Street, and any large-scale development work, hunting Stag in those terms is most beneficial for society but it requires a lot of Trust formally designed into our institutions through laws and regulations shaping society. The benefits of hunting Stag, then, while requiring a sinister world-view of cooperation and Trust, are earned, even when shared by the Fool left behind.

Doubt has a softer side as well. When played out as Fairness, we instantly imagine a level playing field. To be "fair," after all, is to give everyone the same power and place in the structure. No one is cast as the Fool in Fairness. The Great Cake Divide is a procedure credited to John Selfridge (1960) and John Horton Conway (1993), although neither published their discovery.[57] The Great Cake Divide illustrates Fairness near perfection. It's a game without individual hierarchy and has been used successfully to divide cakes, sandwiches and resolve conflict. In this game, the structure is the assurance of fairness. It goes like this: two kids seek to share a piece of cake. Typically, an unknowing parent suffers the task of trying to divide the cake so that neither kid complains they got cheated. Anyone who is a parent, or understands parenting intuitively, knows this never works. If the parent actually cuts the cake and distributes the pieces, every party—including the parent—will feel cheated. But if the parent designed the rules instead, say to make one kid the Divider of the cake and the other kid the Decider with the privilege of choosing first, then the Divider, knowing they'll get what's left will work earnestly to divide the cake as evenly as possible. The Decider, knowing they get first chance to pick the larger piece will study the sections to the nearest crumb. The rules make it possible for everyone in this situation to operate with their own self-interest in mind. The parent announces the game with embedded rules of fair play; the kids each operate with razor sharp skill. And everyone is happy.

It may come as a pleasant surprise, given the characterization of the Great Cake Divide as the ultimate game of Fairness, to learn that the forming of the United States and State's Rights has a lot in common with the Great Cake Divide. After our country won its independence from Great Britain, the task of designing a new governing system fell on the shoulders of a few people—our founding fathers. Alexander Hamilton was one of those founding fathers of the United States. He was also the first Secretary of the Treasury and became our second president.[58] Hamilton was a key supporter of a strong central government. His only point of reference was England and a ruling Monarchy. It had worked for them for centuries, why not borrow it? His vision included a vigorous executive branch to oversee a strong military and a national bank to support a commercial economy and manufacturing, all to become the economic policies of George Washington's administration. Thomas Jefferson, on the other hand, felt the opposite. As a farmer he argued for agrarianism and a smaller government. Jefferson felt the United States had just fought to distance themselves from the monarchy ruling system, so why not take the opportunity to invent something else – especially since State's Rights meant the protection of slavery, the key form of labor for farmers.[59] The two extremes seemed irreconcilable. Along comes James Madison, thinking like the all-knowing parent in the Great Cake Divide. Madison is also one of the founding fathers of the United States and became our fourth U.S. president. Largely credited for promoting the United States Constitution and the Bill of Rights, Madison offers a radical idea. Since each state was unique in terms of production and interests, population size and demands, they would all end up trying different approaches to accomplish similar goals. Some approaches would fail and others would succeed. The experiment that would become America would benefit from the collection of these trials and errors made at the States level.[60] The collection of successes would be advanced to the federal scale with the benefit of having been vetted a few times by the people. The Constitution, like the Great Cake Divide, was a framework, not to be deployed by a single determiner. America, the great project, was founded on the notion that nothing is set in stone at the onset. Rather, trials and errors inform and transform the constitutional framework known as a system for governance.

The doubt created from having someone in charge also has two sides. We meet the Stag Hunt again in any two-person game, agreement or convention. Two rowers in a boat understand the conventions of rowing without giving any promises or assurances to one another. Both rowers can either row or not row. If both rowers row, the outcome is best, just as Rousseau's example of hunting stag together, the team is optimized. However, if one decides not to row, or convention determines only one rower rows, then both must be satisfied with the lesser outcome—similar to the risk averse outcome of hunting hare in the Stag Hunt. The worst possible outcome is when both rowers row opposite of one another causing the boat to either go in circles or, worse yet, capsize.[61]

The dynamic we are witnessing between the two people rowing or the many hunters hunting stag is known as *the Social Contract*.[62] Similar to the classic two-person Prisoner's Dilemma, the Social Contract becomes powerful in a repeat game, a revengeful tit-for-tat, after one player has shown their willingness to break the conventions of cooperation for the greater good and act in self-interest. If two people cooperate in the Prisoner's Dilemma, each is choosing less rather than more. The Prisoner's Dilemma is a classic conflict between individual rationality and mutual benefit.[63] Only in a relationship where you perceive enormous Trust that the other player(s) will also act in mutual benefit will a player choose less over more. It's just not "rational."

The Population Problem extends the complexity of the Social Contract to the next level. First presented by Garrett Hardin in 1968 as the Tragedy of the Commons, Hardin's main point at the time was to call attention to the impossible ability of a finite world to support an infinite growth in population.[64] It was a resource management problem—mathematically, both factors cannot be maximized at once; and biophysically, the calories available per person must decrease as population increases. But the sheepherder story used to illustrate the Tragedy of the Commons sheds light on an even more dangerous fallout shaping the instruments we build to mediate Trust—that of institutional design—the policy framework society creates to manage cooperation, feedback, decision making and consequence. Given, the individuality of rational self-interest, these institutions do not exist a *priori*. They need to be formed. Let me reframe the story here: Two sheepherders share a pasture. They each graze two sheep on the pasture. Then (as I like to tell it), one day one of the sheepherders decides she needs a new Volvo so she adds another sheep to the pasture. The other sheepherder sees this and thinks instantly, "you mean you can do that?" The shot heard 'round the world in that instant is that the tacit understanding of the rules of cooperation in a dynamic setting can be broken without communication or coordination. It's a game changer. And now the effort it will take to unpack what just happened and rethink the rules—possibly also without communication or coordination—will set the tone of every institutional mechanism we design from then on. We must design for the breakdown in Trust. So, the other sheepherder retaliates by also adding another sheep to the pasture—"if she can do it, so can I." Here lies the problem: to ignore the *Shadow of the Future*.[65] Anyone cast as a Social Sucker will not look the other way. A similar demise to the population problem ensues—a tit-for-tat escalation that both damages the carrying capacity of the pasture to support grazing and destroys any opportunity for a reversal of the first decision by the one sheepherder to act in self-interest. Self-interest becomes the gauge, and while the carrying capacity of shared resources held in common remains the same, their value as a divisive tool just multiplied.

Economists model this problem by a curvilinear arc representing the carrying capacity of the environment rising and then declining once the capacity of the environment reaches equilibrium and can no longer stay ahead of demand. Humans, on the other hand, dealing with individual costs equal to individual benefits result in a straight line in the model. Sadly, once the straight line of the humans intersect with the curve of the environment in a state of decline, rational self-interest reveals humans will take out even more if they perceive the resource is threatened. Because, if you don't "get while the gettin's good," there's no guarantee the others using the resource system won't. However, as the model demonstrates, if you go over the point of equilibrium, the system collapses. Benefits minus cost curve show how far we go from a sustainable yield. If you harvest this much over equilibrium, the system is used up and it will collapse and disappear.[66]

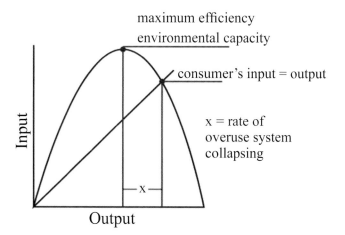

maximum efficiency
environmental capacity

consumer's input = output

x = rate of
overuse system
collapsing

x

Input

Output

*Figure 5. Environment vs Consumer Input
and Output*

Estimating Current Extinction Rates

Population Index = 100 in 1970

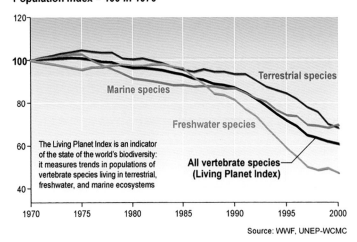

The Living Planet Index is an indicator of the state of the world's biodiversity: it measures trends in populations of vertebrate species living in terrestrial, freshwater, and marine ecosystems

Marine species

Terrestrial species

Freshwater species

All vertebrate species (Living Planet Index)

Source: WWF, UNEP-WCMC

By looking at well-studied focal groups like birds and flowering plants we get an estimate of 10-100 extinctions/million species. This is thought to be an underestimate because the rate of extinction is increasing rapidly, many species are doomed to extinction due to low population size, and many rare species have no doubt gone extinct before they were discovered.

If we include the species on the IUCN Red List of species in danger the estimate goes to 100-1,000/million species. This, too, is an underestimate as the rate of entry onto this list is also accelerating. When that is included the estimate goes to between 1,000-10,000/million species.

The Living Planet Index was updated to include data through 2010. Even though the data show slightly more populations are increasing than declining, the magnitude of the population decline is much greater than that of the increase, resulting in an overall reduction since 1970.

Figure 6. Estimating Current Extinction Rates

In the Sheepherder story, a lack of coordination and communication cause a breakdown in Trust and lead to an escalation of tit-for-tat. The classic Prisoner's Dilemma portrays these costs another way, one that leaves permanent damage to a relationship. The Prisoner's Dilemma has many versions. The one about two friends drives home the point of a severed relationship best: Two friends want to attend a concert of their favorite band in a nearby town on a Sunday night. The trip necessitates they miss a scheduled exam the Monday after the concert. They return Tuesday morning and plead their case with their professor—*a flat tire on the way home from the concert*. The accident caused them a day's delay in getting back home and they were unprepared for the exam. The professor is more than understanding and suggests the two friends plan to take the makeup exam the following Monday giving them ample time to study and prepare. The two friends come to the makeup exam rested, still excited having attended the concert of the decade, and fully prepared for the exam. The professor has them sit in different rooms and hands them the exam. The friends cruise through the exam and turn the test paper over to the final question: "which tire?" Thus, the dilemma. Both students know the other is also taking the same exam. They both have to answer this question. The points for the answer are spelled out as such: If both A and B remain silent (cooperate, cooperate) they each lose 20 points on a 100 point exam for dishonesty. If A betrays B but B remains silent (betray, cooperate), A stands to gain 10 bonus point for honesty and B loses 20 points for dishonesty (and vice versa). If both betray each other (betray, betray), they will be asked to do an additional essay on the Prisoner's Dilemma. The dilemma in the Prisoner's Dilemma is each person has to make a decision without consulting with the other. They each have complete information about the situation, but incomplete information about what the other will do.

In the classic Prisoner's Dilemma, the payoff matrix looks like this:

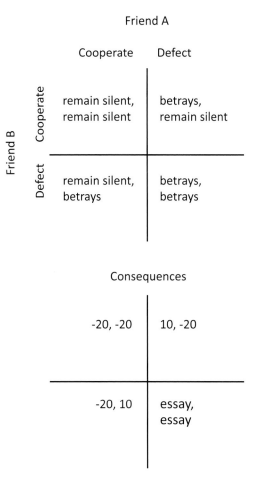

Figure 7. Prisoner's Dilemma Payoff Matrix

Because betraying a friend with the chance the friend won't betray you offers a higher reward, and one can rationalize the other will think the same way; but because any choice involving betrayal will involve an end to the friendship, the decision is never easy. The Prisoner's Dilemma has been a source of lengthy scholarly research and has been used as a model for real world situations involving cooperative and strategic behavior. Taken to the next level, the Tragedy of the Commons is a repeat Prisoner's Dilemma that gets us closer to the problems associated with the Social Contract.

Thomas Hobbes, who originated the *Leviathan* in 1651, was an English philosopher with the view that the state of nature of human beings would be living in a constant state of competitiveness and violence.[67] He felt the only way to control this violent nature was to form institutions such as political stratification designed to keep people in control. Garrett Hardin, who authored *The Tragedy of the Commons*, held a similar ecological view of people in competition. Hardin claimed that people, when left to their own devices, will ultimately over-exploit their environment.

Research of human-environment relations comparing pre-industrial societies with post-industrial societies require both empirical and theoretical effort. Pre-industrial societies were more reliant on their immediate environment. Environmental determinism claims cultures are completely shaped by their environments and assumes all cultures develop the same way if in the same environmental area.[68] In Post-Industrial societies, on the other hand, theories are also indelibly linked to technologies. Therefore, contemporary thinkers cannot theorize pre-industrial societies without acknowledging their own post-industrial, technological, bias. My Fairness Framework takes into account three ways environmental complexity and cultural complexity interact. The first is to observe the criticalness of the shared Commons on a community's livelihood and economic stability. The second is to observe the institutions communities create to manage these shared environments. The third is to observe the patterns of human behavior created from different self-interested practices. The theory assumes self-interest is not always all bad. Competition in the example of the opportunity-individual nexus of entrepreneurialism allows for good things to come of self-interested entrepreneurial exploits, i.e., Apple and Tesla, to name a few.

What I take from *The Tragedy of the Commons* by Thomas Hobbes and David Hume is not so much that humans will exploit their environment, because they will. But, rather the way it sets into motion the mistake of ignoring the *Shadow of the Future* in a repeat Prisoner's Dilemma game. If there were only one move, we might be able to get away with it. As the saying goes, "what happens in Vegas stays in Vegas." But there is no single move. There is a future, even after Vegas. Casting a Social Sucker of the cooperative actor, simply because that actor chooses to not exploit the situation (here environment broadly defined as in situation/site), is a major crimp in the armor of The Social Contract. The Social Sucker will seek revenge to even the score. It's that kind of retaliatory act that pits the environment at risk.

To analyze the *Shadow of the Future*, we start with the theory of indefinite repeated games. In a repeated game, the Fool's strategy (acting in self-interest, a player always defects) is to *Always Defect*. Hobbes demonstrates that if someone always defects, others will not cooperate with them.[69] Those who initially cooperate but who later retaliate, as Hobbes suggests against defectors, have a *Trigger* strategy. If the Fool's two strategies are *Always Defect* and *Trigger* in a repeated game, the *Shadow of the Future* will transform the two-person Prisoner's Dilemma into the multi-person Stag Hunt. Recall, the Stag Hunt has a way of coercing the other hunters to hunt the same way. Therefore, for a strategy to be effective *against* a Fool (someone who's been made a Social Sucker for cooperating), the Fool must believe that the others are not Fools (remember, in the Stag Hunt, hunting hare or hunting stag are equilibria—it's always best if you hunt what the group is hunting). Those who play it safe (withdraw their money after the stock market takes a down turn) will always choose *Always Defect*. The *Trigger* move in Shadow of the Future, therefore, has transformed the dilemma of not knowing how the other will act in the Prisoner's Dilemma (remember the two friends) into a cooperative Stag Hunt. Group-Think takes over.[70] The Social Contract, then, can be adopted and modified for mutual benefit as seen in a multi-person Stag Hunt. There will always be more risk for the person(s) devoting energy to instituting the new Social Contract. If people see the new move and follow it, the risk was worth it. If people see the new move and ignore it, the risk becomes a loss.

The problem of instituting or improving the Social Contract can be thought of as the problem of moving from riskless Hunt Hare equilibrium to the risky but rewarding Hunt Stag equilibrium. So how do we get from the Hunt Hare equilibrium to the Hunt Stag equilibrium? According to the multi-person Stag Hunt game, it is best to do what all the others are doing. There is no payoff for being a renegade. It agrees with Hume's contention that a thousand-person stag hunt is more difficult to achieve than a two-person stag hunt. The problem of Trust is multiplied. So, from the standpoint of a rational choice, there will be no change in the status quo. According to Hobbes and Hardin, given the fallout from the Prisoner's Dilemma and the inability for two people to turn broken Trust around, an all-knowing external agent needs to step in. We will walk through this in the next chapter by revisiting five games outlined in Elinor Ostrom's *Governing the Commons*. I have layered some additional observations onto her games as I present my own Fairness Framework. But for now, it is enough to say, what deserves more close scrutiny in Hobbes' and Hardin's view of the Social Contract is in how they view that initial Cheat. Perhaps we can applaud the fact that we live in a time when we are no longer surprised by people's bad behavior. And, in fact, more and more the Cheat is expected (and even invited as in asking expert outsiders to "break" a new game or code or program). Here, our lack of surprise in the Cheat makes us resilient and willing to modify the Social Contract. And, here's a surprise, we just might see why re-framing the Cheat is a key approach to addressing society's larger structural issues.

Nature, the genome of diversity

The resiliency of natural systems ecologies is threatened not so much by population growth or demographics change but by the intrusion of policy-decisions made by those populations affecting precious ecosystems around the world. The diminishing per-capita size of the farming communities in North Dakota where I grew up is a great case in point. Without understanding the effect of advancing till agriculture around the world, for example, and building access roads to those sites, we essentially cut, carve, erase and generally threaten critical habitats. The dilemma is that the loss of species threatens human survival due to a loss of resistance to disease spread. Because all domesticated organisms originated from wild species such as wheat, corn, goats, cattle, and chickens that taken from the wild each exhibited considerable gene diversity within its own ranks. Such genetic diversity was extremely important to survival of the species because it ensured the existence of strains with resistance to certain stresses in the environment such as disease and drought. *Natural systems agriculture* that retains genetic diversity has been reconstructed through the laudatory efforts of organizations like the Land Institute.[71] Their effort to reimagine the four synchronous grasses comprising natural systems agriculture of the tall grass prairie is especially fascinating. The four grasses mix includes a warm-season grass, a cool-season grass, a legume, and a composite. The warm-season grass survives a drought while a cool-season grass survives a rain out. Legumes transform the elements from the air and soil into nutrients for the plant and the composites rebuild the soil in a birth-to-death cycle. The scientists at the Land Institute engineered the mix in hopes of discovering the same four synchronous grasses in any ecosystem—the rainforest, the prairie, the mountains, and cities. The goal was to swap out equivalent plants suitable for food production in that climate without disrupting the relationship of these "sister" grasses in any particular ecosystem. In testing the crop, however, the first year nothing bloomed. The scientists rechecked their formulas. Everything should have worked. The second year, again, nothing bloomed. The third year the same. Scientists pondered the problem, yet the science seemed flawless. Finally, the fourth year, the field erupted in the perfect crop of synchronous grass-es. What hadn't been factored in was the time the entire eco-system needed to extend the root system, animate the subsoil community, and attract the right pollinators. In developing the complexity necessary for a resilient perennial polyculture, the challenge facing agronomists and ecologists has always been to restore the native ecology of the tall-grass prairie and the eco-logical services that it provides in such a way that the forage and food requirements of humanity are still met. Complexity in the design and establishment of natural systems agriculture calls upon the characterization and subsequent domestication of native plant species along with the elucidation of the eco-logical principles that govern their *intelligence architectures* in perennial mixtures. We need more people in the world who understand these principles.

Elinor Ostrom was one of those people. She is also one of my heroes. I've been inspired by her book *Governing the Com-mons: The Evolution of Institutions for Collective Action* and have used it as a prime text in my graduate seminar since 2005. Ostrom was the first woman to be awarded the Nobel Prize for Economic Sciences.[72] She received the 2009 Nobel Prize for her groundbreaking research demonstrating ordinary people are capable of creating rules and institutions supporting sus-tainable and fair management of shared and finite resources. She died June 12, 2012. Her husband, Vincent Ostrom, died 17 days later, on June 29, 2012. Elinor used game theory to analyze collective action situations around the world. Her five games demonstrate the need for nested enterprises ranging from self-organized grassroots institutions to those regulated by a central government. Here are her five games:

The Tragedy of the Commons, also called the Hardin herder game, has been formalized as a prisoner's dilemma (PD) game to look like this: using a scale of 0-10 profit units for each play-er, if both players cooperate (cooperate, cooperate), the payoff is (10, 10). But, as we see in the herder story, each player has a dominant strategy—to defect—which adds a third sheep to the pasture. Since there is yet no way of policing this choice, each player is always better off choosing that strategy no matter what the other player chooses (**defect**, cooperate) results in (**11**, -1) or (cooperate, **defect**) results in (-1, **11**) depending on which player (P1 or P2) defects. When they both choose this strategy, however, the outcome is not Pareto-optimal (0, 0). A Pareto-op-timal outcome occurs when at least one player is able to choose the most preferred outcome over the other player. In a two-per-son PD, both players would prefer the (cooperate, cooperate) outcome to the (defect, defect) outcome. Since (defect, defect) results in a (0, 0) equilibrium, the outcome of a dominant strate-gy (always defect) in a PD is Pareto-inferior.[73]

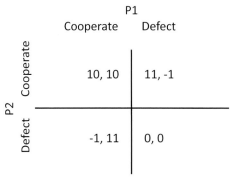

Figure 8. Game 1 Payoff Matrix

What is fascinating about the prisoner's dilemma is the notion that it is impossible for rational beings to cooperate. This bears directly on fundamental issues in ethics and political philosophy. It threatens the foundations of social science and presents paradoxes commanding a central position in philosophical discussions.

Key for me is the impact on the Social Contract after that initial betrayal of Trust. As soon as a player has indicated they are willing to act in self-interest ("you mean you can do that?"), Trust breaks down. Imagine this as an epiphany we call Game 1. The resultant tit-for-tat takes us instantly to (defect, defect) or (0, 0) in repeat games (Game 1.1, 1.2, 1.3, etc.), until finally we need another Game.

Ophuls,[74] portrays a new tragedy, "because of the tragedy of the commons, environmental problems cannot be solved through cooperation ... and the rationale for government with major coercive powers is overwhelming." Therefore, an external agent, the "Leviathan,"[75] would have to intervene. Hardin himself also conceded, "if ruin is to be avoided in a crowded world, people must be responsive to a coercive force outside their individual psyches, a 'Leviathan,' to use Hobbes's term."[76] Here, Ostrom modifies the Hardin herder game using the recommendation for a central authority above to become Game 2.[77] An external agent will represent centralized control and decide on a grazing strategy after considering all the best possible outcomes for the situation. The external agent will decide who can use the pasture, when they can use it, and how many animals can graze on it. For this external agent to be "perfect," however, there will be a cost to each of the herders. The external agent will need to become familiar enough with the carrying capacity of the pasture and be able to monitor the situation expertly as to never miss a Cheat. And if there is a Cheat, the external agent must be able to understand the dynamics well enough to know how to sanction bad behavior and how to reward good behavior in order to safeguard the future of the

pasture. The assumption with Game 2 modified this way is that there *IS* such a thing as a perfect external agent. And now the costs to each sheepherder to employ such a perfect external agent have to be factored into the benefits for choosing the optimal strategy (defect, cooperate) is really (9, -1) to reflect both the additional cost of the carrying capacity of the pasture and the cost of paying for the external agent. For both players to choose their dominant strategy (defect, defect), the payoff is now (-2, -2). So, while the payoff for cooperating remains the same (10, 10), the reward for acting in self-interest (defect) with an all-knowing agent watching over your shoulder is reduced to nine and the cost of both players choosing their dominant strategy (defect, defect) is worse (-2, -2).[78]
Now the payoff matrix looks like this:

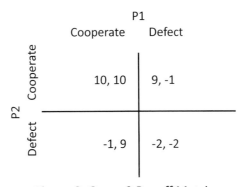

Figure 8. Game 2 Payoff Matrix

Unfortunately, we have very few lessons from history to show us humans can learn our lesson and go back to square one (cooperate, cooperate) until we've exhausted all other options to defect. Turning back from Game 2 to Game 1 at this point would be wise, but people are irrational. In fact, pride and recovering from being made the Social Sucker is a perfectly rational motivation to keep the games in play in order to recover dignity through retaliation. Acting irrationally is so predictably rational, in fact, it is essential to game theory strategy. Also, the fallacy in the illustrations so far is, first, there is no such thing as a perfect external agent. And second, since Trust has been broken with that original Cheat, and a Social Sucker has been made of the cooperating player, it is too soon to ask that player to forgive all debt and start over. Rebuilding Trust takes some new insights to put the Cheat in perspective. So, we play on.

In the next section, INDETERMINACY, I break down three more games before we arrive at an understanding of the real costs of a lack of coordination and cooperation. And we actually begin to see some opportunities for being invested in sloppy institutional design. Ultimately, we arrive at a new way to reform the Social Contract, one that anticipates, even *counts on*, the other player to cheat.

INDETERMINACY

INDETERMINACY

Impossible to plot culture

I was a freshman in architecture when Michael Graves, an influential Postmodern architect, presented his Fargo-Moorhead Cultural Bridge to a group of students and faculty.[79] He explained "the river was the keystone." Signifying the formidable presence of this wide bank-less, edge-less Red River of the North to members of this agricultural community with this metaphor seemed instantly accurate. The keystone is the stone or brick at the top of an arch placed to keep the entire formation in balance. I thought Graves was spot-on with that metaphor. It was consistent with the way comedian Joan Rivers delightfully described the Plains as "being so flat you could see your relatives coming six months out." Michael Graves drew from the natural forces of that river to either flood or to fortify to enrich the indeterminate reading of his work. Indeterminacy and complexity have always been visionary images for Modern and Postmodern Movements. *The Skyscraper Theorem* of 1909 describes indeterminacy through the ideal performance of the skyscraper: a slender steel structure supports 84 horizontal planes, all the size of the original plot. Each of the artificial levels is treated as an isolated site, as if the others did not exist. In *Delirious New York*[80] architect Rem Koolhaus explains, "This indeterminacy means that a particular site can no longer be matched with any single predetermined purpose. From now on each metropolitan lot accommodates—in theory at least—an unforeseeable and unstable combination of simultaneous activities ... it has become impossible to "plot culture."[81] Early work contributing to thinking about indeterminacy in this way can be traced back to Ludwig von Bertalanffy (1901-1972), an important theoretical biologist researching comparative physiology, biophysics, cancer, psychology and philosophy. Working with a humanistic worldview, he was keenly critical of the machine metaphor (if-then statements) for explaining existence. His main goal was to unite metabolism, growth, morphogenesis and sense physiology toward a methodology of science known as his *General Systems Theory* (GST). GST's representation of a set of interrelated components made the Skyscraper Theorem a viable premise. Recoverable copies of the original lot below accommodate immense possibility in the sky.

Alongside GST, *Information Theory* championed by C. E. Shannon, acknowledged the brain is designed to work well with enormous amounts of synchronous information. A single channel can contain multiple messages without mutual interference. Multiple signals or sine waves can be bundled together and transmitted at one end (referred to as "many-to-one") and then separated again at the receiving end.[82] In brain terms, a single neuron can process not only one signal but also multiple complex ideas about the world presented to it at any time.

C. E. Shannon's work on the signal-to-noise ratio brought intelligence architectures forward. The fundamental problem was not one of engineering, but of meaning constructed by the receiver. The fact that the actual message was to be selected from a larger set of possible messages, the system had to be designed to operate for each possible selection. Engineering this possibility means operating in terms that can be scalable and random. Possibly lost in the message of the Modern Movement, Robert Venturi (*Complexity and Contradiction*) brought *postmodern complexity* back to architecture. "The problem with architecture and urbanism," Venturi claims, "is that it is too reductive. By carefully limiting the problems it would solve, modern architecture produced solutions that were pure, but boring. As a result, modern architecture is not on a level with modern science, poetry, or art, all of which recognize complexity and contraction."[83] On par with Shannon's Information Theory, Venturi argues, "Inclusiveness produces positive artistic tension and leads to a rich condition of multiple interpretations."[84] If only the Social Contract could manage the indeterminacy called up by enormous diversity.

In Ostrom's Game 2 above, we left off with the realization that there is no such thing as a perfect external agent. Factoring in the diversity challenge that comes with incomplete information—the central agent may have complete information about the carrying capacity of the pasture, but incomplete information about the particular behaviors of the herders (and vice versa). The central agent consequently makes an error in actions towards the herders or miscalculates the measures needed to protect the pasture. Without valid or reliable information, rewards may also be improperly administered or imposed at the wrong time. Assumptions about the accuracy of information, the monitoring capabilities, the reliability of sanctioning and rewarding leave a probability of error we must account for. In Ostrom's description, the central agency punishes uncooperative behavior (the correct response) with a probability of y. The central agent fails to punish uncooperative behavior (the wrong response) with a probability of $1-y$. Other ways the central agent can fail is to punish cooperative behavior (the wrong response) with a probability of $1-x$ and rewards cooperative behavior (the correct response) with a probability of x. If a central agent with complete information (Game 2) were indeed perfect, then $x=0$ (cooperation) and $y = 1$ (defection). But if the central agent does not have complete information and imposes both types of sanctions incorrectly, we see a probability of now ($x = 0.3$, $y = 0.7$). Therefore, to factor in the probability of this kind of error, now (cooperate, cooperate) isn't a full (10, 10), but rather a (10 - 2x, 10 - 2x), and (defect, cooperate) is (11 - 2y, -1 - 2x), and (cooperate, defect) is (-1 - 2x, 11 - 2y), and finally (defect, defect) is (-2y, -2y).[85]

Factoring in the probability that there is no perfect agent, we get a more realistic picture in, what is now, Game 3. The formulas look like this:

(cooperate, cooperate) is (10 - 2x, 10 - 2x), and
(defect, cooperate) is (11 - 2y, -1 - 2x), alternately
(cooperate, defect) is (-1 - 2x, 11 - 2y), finally
(defect, defect) is (-2y, -2y)

So, with complete information, (x = 0, y = 1), the payoff equation results are:
10 - 2(0) = 10, 11 - 2(1) = 9, -1 - 2(1) = -1 -2(1) = -2
And the payoff matrix looks like this for Game 2:

	C	D
C	10, 10	9, -1
D	-1, 9	-2, -2

Figure 9. Game 2 with Complete Information

With incomplete information, (x = 0.3, y = 0.7), the payoff equation results are:
10-2(0.3)=9.4, 11-2(0.7)=9.6,-1-2(0.7)=-1.6, -1 -2(0.7)=-1.4
And the payoff matrix looks like this for Game 3:

	C	D
C	9.4, 9.4	9.6, -1.6
D	-1.6, 9.6	-1.4, -1.4

Figure 10. Game 3 with Incomplete Information

I call the next game "the Watcher of the Watcher"—which adds a layer of bureaucracy with the additional oversight. In my view, Game 4 is simply more of Game 3 but higher up in the regulation ladder. We can also imagine there could be layers of institutional costs in both Game 3 and Game 4 (3.1, 3.2, etc., and 4.1, 4.2, etc.). It isn't hard to see the equilibrium of the regulated game (defect, defect) has a lower value than that of the unregulated game.[86]

-2, -2 for (defect, defect) in Game 2 under the perfect agent,
 and -1.4, -1.4 for (defect, defect) in Game 3 and 4 under the imperfect agent.

From this we conclude, as a non-cooperative player looking to advantage the system, we will always do better when institutions are poorly designed and unregulated. Presented another way—and this is critical—the environment, the shared pasture, is slowly and inevitably incrementally threatened more under conditions of poorly designed institutions and unregulated behavior leading to an individual's dominant strategy to defect. Designed to make the environment a Social Sucker, if you are the defector looking for an opportunity where someone is looking the other way, the individual—opportunity nexus theory of entrepreneurialism supports this conclusion as well. Opportunities are not a-*priori*, waiting to be discovered. No, there needs to be a circumstance where an individual sees an opportunity (the need for widgets) and the environment is just right (no tax on widgets; no competition for widgets; no one has figured out the monopoly) to create the right entrepreneurial move. Given, the environment has no rights under the Constitution of the United States, and given, the more bureaucracy we try layer onto the system the more likely an individual with an incentive to defect will find an opportunity to do so, how do we design an institutional framework where the environment isn't always the Social Sucker and where getting caught is not viewed as cheating? Rather, how can cheating be treated as new information on how the system works, with the end goal of protecting the shared pasture from self-interest?

Generative and fanciful

Douglas Hofstadter in *Godel, Escher, Bach: An Eternal Golden Braid* describes the musical canon as a puzzle game made popular in the day of Frederick the Great, King of Prussia.[87] Johann Sebastian Bach wrote ten canons in the *Musical Offering* for King Frederick.[88] The canon lends itself to this kind of system/puzzle because the theme is played against itself. The canon introduces its single theme along with some tricky hints and the canon theme is to be "discovered" by the listener. A round is a canon. "Three Blind Mice" and "Row, Row, Row Your Boat" are simple canons. Canons use time (staggered copies) and pitch (harmonic when voices overlap) and complexity (to invert the original theme below the copy), yet all the information about the original theme is always recoverable from any of the copies. This kind of transformation is called *an isomorphism* and contributes significantly to our understanding of similarities in form, structure or correspondences in identity of systems. A more complex musical puzzle is a fugue. The Tallis Scholars directed by Peter Phillips present "Spem in alium," a 40-voice motet.[89] I hope readers will go to the YouTube link and listen to the Tallis Scholars sing this piece. The telltale sign of this fugue is the way it begins: a single voice sings the theme. When the first voice completes a phrase, it continues with a secondary theme while the second voice and then the third, the fourth, and so on, up to the full 40 voices, enter in harmony with some accompaniment of the counter-subject in some other voice. When all 40 voices have arrived in "Spem in alium," the piece is magical, living well beyond its end because we have been introduced to an indeterminate "theme" not a song. The fanciful and generative accomplishment of the canon or fugue theme as a system is that it uses the counter-subject to provide rhythmic, harmonic and melodic contrasts to the subject. Unlike a point/counterpoint deterministic system in debate to expose difference, *the canon and the fugue* are oppor-tunistic in their intent to align similarities. The system as theme is played against itself making diversity into harmonic sustain-ability. Graphic designers are masters of designing for probability like witnessed in the canon and the fugue. Similarly, theoretical architects Bernard Cache and Greg Lynn working with digital fab-rication have explored the indeterminacy of commands such as fold, strand, lattice, shred, branch, flower, and blob to arrive at a generative, non-reductive architecture.[90] Greg Lynn's Embryonic House, for example, envisions each family's program or situation as having its own inherent genomic sequence called up in the forming of the architecture.[91] Like an algorithm for moving from *the fringe to the center* it simply involves rules about turning in-flexible systems of thought, society, and policy into intelligent and flexible systems of being. Like the canon and the fugue, the isomorphism, the HGP, the basic theme is recoverable from one copy to the next. But the end is not deterministic.

Poro[U.S. Border]s: the place of policy

The following research case study targets the paradigm where the centrality of disease and medicine in the management of a healthier global community receives much attention, especially with regard to transmissible or vaccine preventable diseases. In fact, between 2006 and 2007 alone, 35 billion dollars targeted global health research and delivery. However, the role of dis-ease management extends well beyond issues of individual hu-man health to encompass larger geopolitical questions of place as a means and an emblem of effective health care delivery. Policy resistance has been defined as the tendency for inter-ventions to be defeated by the system's own response to the intervention itself.[92] Health policy design, then, given its history of disease management as a function of nations bounded by borders is hardly effective in a world that is hardly static and highly mobile. So, when we experience global population mo-bility, displacement from reliable social networks, a disease ep-idemic, conflict or environmental disaster, what happens to the health of the public under these conditions of flux and stress? And what other systems absorb the shocks where health poli-cy seems unresponsive? And how might feedback from these resilient systems inform and further transform global health frameworks for more effective implementation? A healthier health commons, viewed here as a Common Pool Resource (CPR) system, is the goal of this project. The U.S.-Mexico border and a close study characterizing the resilience of local Colonias provides a context for critical analysis of community dynamics and resilient grassroots systems amplified by unique conditions of international mobility, social/political uncertainty, and economic disparity. This collaborative and interdisciplinary work developed an original thesis about the ways in which 18th and 19th century geopolitical understanding of disease and colonization powerfully shaped our current global health framework. In addition, the innovative mathematical and system modeling and institutional mapping presented a foundational analysis to begin to understand a shifting paradigm in global disease management for characteristic of a world of porous borders.

. . . . . .

Darla V. Lindberg

. . . . . .

Poro[U.S. Border]s: the place of policy
Selected images were part of a public lecture presented on December 3, 2010 outlining the trajectory of a rich collaborative and interdisciplinary research funded by a three-year National Institutes of Health and Fogarty International Center grant. Central to the work is my Fairness Framework, a model I developed for Commons + Institutions + Human Behavior systems design.

Dedicated to the memory of Elinor Ostrom (1933-2012), Nobel Prize in Economic Science. 2009.

Ostrom was not trained as an economist, but as a social sci-entist—a factor that has been credited to her outside-the-box approach to economics. She inspired my work to make sense of the feedback processes among individuals, the institutions we create and the effectiveness of those institutions to keep pace with urban, environmental and ecological conditions of constant change and flux. The transferability of the model to an array of Case Study research highlights the role design thinking plays in the policy arena. The work serves as a power-ful medium for analyzing the confluence of social, economic, political, and ecological systems giving form and relevance to cities, communities, and significantly to human issues of living and well-being affected by economic and environmental policy.

Poro[US Border]s: the place of policy
not without the complex mechanics of policy beyond the discipline

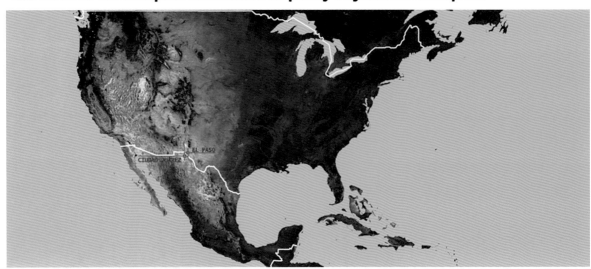

Pathologies of Power: Health, Human Rights, and the New War on the Poor by Paul Farmer is a plea for a working definition of human rights that would not neglect the most basic rights of all: food, shelter, and health. "The capacity to suffer is, clearly, a part of being human. But not all suffering is equivalent. It is possible to speak of extreme human suffering, and an inordinate share of this sort of pain is currently endured by those living in poverty."

The poor are the chief victims of structural violence—a form of violence based on the systematic ways in which a given social structure or institution harms people by preventing them from meeting their basic needs.

When social status denies access to social progress
Time to rethink institutional design

"A third of the 2 Billion people in the developing countries are suffering from malnutrition. Twenty-five per cent of their children die before their fifth birthday. Less than 10 per cent of the 15 million children who died this year had been vaccinated against the six most common and dangerous children's diseases. Vaccinating every child costs £3 per child. But not doing so costs us five million lives a year." (Farmer)

These are classic examples of *structural violence*. Structural violence is visited upon all those whose social status denies them access to the fruits of scientific and social progress. Farmer argues neither culture nor pure individual will is at fault; rather, historically given processes and mechanics constrain individual agency.

Global Appeals to Policy Resistance:

Because we thought it was about resource management from the top down, Science argued for money in 2006...

The New World of Global Health
January 2006

A cadre of deep-pocketed, impassioned players committed more than $35 billion to fight the diseases of the world's poor

Since 1999 Bill and Melinda Gates Foundation $6 billion - roughly the budget of the World Health Organization (WHO) during the same time to battle HIV/AIDS, malaria, tuberculosis, and other long under-funded diseases

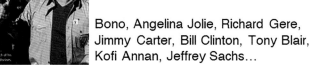

...plus a half dozen other massive new efforts, matinee idols and world leaders

Bono, Angelina Jolie, Richard Gere, Jimmy Carter, Bill Clinton, Tony Blair, Kofi Annan, Jeffrey Sachs...

Global Appeals to Policy Resistance:
Missing the Target...treatment *not* getting to the people who needed it most

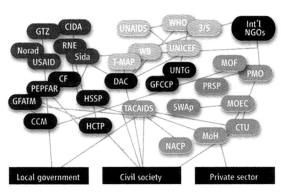

Relationships Between Various Stakeholders in Tanzania

United Nations		Coordinating committees
Bilateral aid		Plans and programs
Drug-delivery programs		IMF/World Bank
Tanzanian government		Nongovernmental organizations

Thirty's a crowd. A confusing cluster of efforts aims to help Tanzania with its HIV/AIDS epidemic.

The biggest AIDS donor, **Global Fund,** country owned and inclusive claiming transparency and accountability as a means to avoid top-down approaches to delivery.

Aidspan, a New York-based watchdog of Global Fund, "complete autonomy comes at a steep price. No one is working together."

Missing the Target, by 600 treatment activists, "a much more systematic approach to designing accountability, such as setting goals, measuring progress, and assessing and addressing barriers is needed. There needs to be an implementation architecture."

Because collective decisions favor the status quo

Society has a bias towards stability – but life is rarely stable and highly mobile

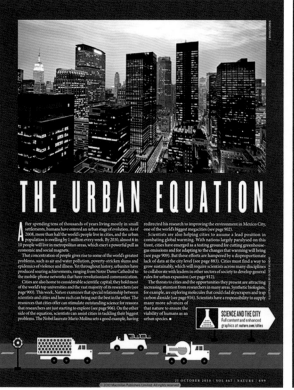

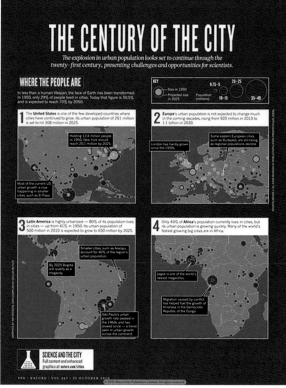

Science Magazine: The New World of Global Health, January 2006, described how a cadre of deep-pocketed, impassioned players committed more than $35 billion to fight the diseases of the world's poor. A year later. "Missing the Target" in Science Magazine reported "a much more systematic approach to designing accountability, such as setting goals, measuring progress, and assessing and addressing barriers is needed. There needs to be an implementation architecture."

Understanding a shifting paradigm
In institutional design more characteristic of a world of porous borders

Therefore,
A healthier health commons, viewed here as a Common Pool Resource (CPR) system, is the goal of this project. Our collaborative work develops an original thesis about the ways in which 18th and 19th century geopolitical understanding of disease and colonization powerfully shape our current global health framework. We need a paradigm shift.
Mathematical and systems modeling and institutional mapping present a foundational analysis to begin to understand a shifting paradigm in global disease management more characteristic of a world of porous borders.

The U.S.-Mexico border provides a context for critical analysis of community dynamics and resilient grassroots systems amplified by unique conditions of international mobility, social/political uncertainty, and economic disparity.

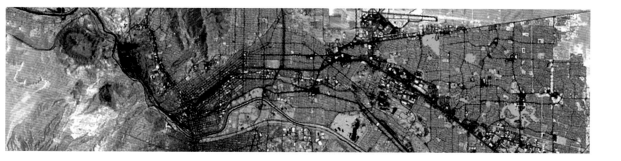

"For most of us, design is invisible… In fact, the secret ambition of design is to become invisible, to be taken up into the culture, absorbed into the background. The highest order of success in design is to achieve ubiquity. The automobile, the freeway, the airplane, the cell phone, the air conditioner, the high-rise…have achieved design nirvana. They are no longer considered unnatural. Most of the time, we live our lives within these invisible systems, blissfully unaware of the artificial life, the intensely designed infrastructures that support them. When systems fail – through accidents, disasters, crisis – we become temporarily conscious of the extraordinary force and power of design, and the effects that it generates. Every accident provides a brief moment of awareness of real life, what is actually happening, and our dependence on the underlying systems of design." ----Bruce Mau

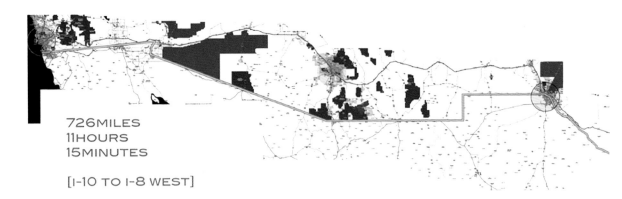

726MILES
11HOURS
15MINUTES

[I-10 TO I-8 WEST]

Team

Darla Lindberg, Primary Investigator
Associate Professor, Architecture
Rachel Smith, Co-Primary Investigator
Assistant Professor, Communications
Tim Reluga, Investigator
Assistant Professor, Mathematics
Mary Poss, Senior Researcher
Professor, Epidemiology Biology
Jill Findeis, Senior Researcher
Professor, Demography
Jing Li, Post-Doc
EPIDEMIOLOGICAL MATHEMATICS

Acknowledgements

Anthony Catanzaro
Matthew Gindlesperger
Adam Longenbach
Danielle Rivera
Ashley Bryan
Gina DeLeon
David Mosemann
Barbara Cutler
Scott Tucker

CIDD (Center for Infectious Disease Dynamics)
Exploratory/Development Grant
Department of Health and Human Services
NATIONAL INSTITUTES OF HEALTH
FOGARTY INTERNATIONAL CENTER
Grant Number: 1R21TW008378-01

Presented by Darla Lindberg ---- December 3, 2010

Herzog & De Meuron

Reveal unfamiliar or unknown relationships by utilizing innovative materials. They cite Joseph Beuys, a German performance artist, installation artist, art theorist and pedagogue as an enduring artistic inspiration. Beuys has extensive work grounded in concepts of humanism, social philosophy, and the idea of social sculpture, for which he claimed a creative, participatory role in shaping society and politics.

Thom Mayne

Morphosis design philosophy develops from an interest in producing work with a meaning that can be understood by absorbing the culture for which it was made. Such notion is in opposition to typical architectural philosophies which overlay meaning from outside influences and are distant from the question at hand.

Better theories to help us think about systems
Because the locus of questions reside in the integration of systems

Theoretical underpinning to this approach: Complexity and General Systems Theory (GST)

Thinking in complexity is an essential paradigm for comprehending the capacity of huge numbers of unique phenomena acting in synergetic relation.

Characteristics of complexity thinking explain the nonlinear, indeterminate and irreducible complex systems linking the food chain to disease spread to global economics.

General Systems Theory is the study of the organization of phenomena in relation, but what is important is not that a relation exists but that the structural similarities for expression, metabolism and interaction inherent to a resilient system, are not lost in the transformation resulting from that relation. GST seeks to explain the physics of how systems work in real life.

The locus of rich questions, then, resides in the relation, the seam, the border, the dynamics and impacts where all systems collide.

Darla V. Lindberg

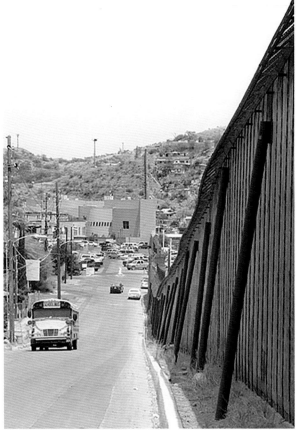

For me, the goal of architecture to tell us as much about the situation that induced the giving as anything about its own technical or aesthetic craft.

So that means building the incredible back-story and then reacting to that using the tools and skills of the inherited and debated legacy of architecture.

US side of the U.S.-Mexico border at Nogales, Arizona

Examples of Complexity Thinking and Systems Theory
The inventor of DDT was awarded a Nobel Prize

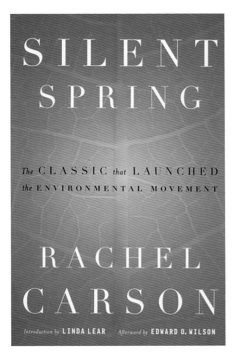

Available for civilian use in 1945, DDT was the most powerful pesticide the world had ever known.

Biologist Rachel Carson's *Silent Spring* (1964) was one of the landmark books of the 20th century tackling the issues of DDT.

Presented as literature rather than scientific report, her work caught the attention of the public and President John F. Kennedy.

Galvanizing the vulnerability of nature to human intervention her work set the stage for the environment movement.

Examples of Complexity Thinking and Systems Theory
Prior to the emergence of germ theory in the 1870s

ANCIENT HISTORY   MIDDLE AGES

1500BC The book of Leviticus deals with personal and community responsibilities and included guidance regarding the cleanliness of body, sexual health behaviors, protection against contagious diseases and the isolation of lepers.

500s End of Roman ideology, paradigm to associate sickness with sin begins, thought to have spiritual causes and solutions. Little consideration for environment and people as disease transmitters

380BC Hippocrates is credited with the founding of western medicine with the book *On Airs, Waters, and Places*

1348 black plague kills 2/3 of people in major european cities causing radical changes in health research and policy

Examples of Complexity Thinking and Systems Theory
The dominant model of disease spread was not of contamination

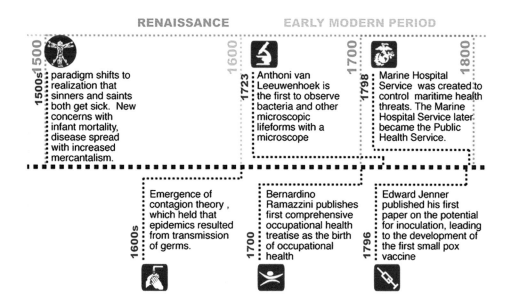

RENAISSANCE   EARLY MODERN PERIOD

1500s
paradigm shifts to realization that sinners and saints both get sick. New concerns with infant mortality, disease spread with increased mercantalism.

1723
Anthoni van Leeuwenhoek is the first to observe bacteria and other microscopic lifeforms with a microscope

1798
Marine Hospital Service was created to control maritime health threats. The Marine Hospital Service later became the Public Health Service.

1600s
Emergence of contagion theory, which held that epidemics resulted from transmission of germs.

1700
Bernardino Ramazzini publishes first comprehensive occupational health treatise as the birth of occupational health

1796
Edward Jenner published his first paper on the potential for inoculation, leading to the development of the first small pox vaccine

Examples of Complexity Thinking and Systems Theory
That disease could travel from sources other than the air

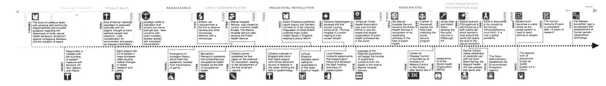

INDUSTRIAL REVOLUTION

1800 ————————————————————————————— **1900**

1843 Edwin Chadwick publishes report *Inquiry into Sanitary Conditions of the Laboring Population of Great Britain* outlining major public health issues in England leading to policy reform.

1860 Florence Nightengale develops the first secular nursing school at St. Thomas Hospital in London, helping to train nurses herself

1872  American Public Health Association was was founded. APHA is now the oldest and largest organization of public health professionals in the world.

1831 Cholera outbreak in England kills more than black plague, John Snow discovers source of disease in city water, birthing the field of epidemiology

1850 Lemual Shattuck releases report calling for assemblance of first state board of health

1864 Louis Pasteur conducts experiments that support germ theory and develops the flash heating technique of pasteurization

1878 passage of the National Quarantine Act began the transfer of quarantine functions from the states to the federal Marine Hospital Service

Examples of Complexity Thinking and Systems Theory
Medical cartography put "disease on the map"

Adolph Muhry's Global Disease Map 1856

Examples of Complexity Thinking and Systems Theory
The central tenet that a geographical link existed between disease & place – the plague and leprosy came from the "East"

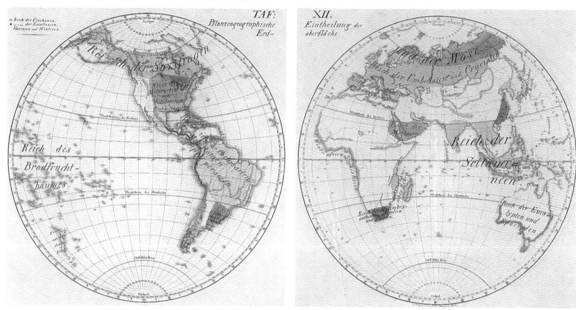

Humboldtian Representations in Medical Cartography
Contributed to views on environmental determinism of 19th century

Nicolaas A. Rupke and Karen E. Wonders

Examples of Complexity Thinking and Systems Theory
Imagining disease was very much a part of imagining place

MODERN ERA

POST-MODERN ERA /
INFORMATION AGE

1900 — **1970** — **2000**

1912 the Marine Hospital Service became the Public Health Service in recognition of its expanding activities in the field of public health.

1935 Franklin D. Roosevelt passes the New Deal instituting the social security program

1954 Jonas Salk and Albert Sabin develop the first polio vaccine in Pittsburgh, PA

1960 Searle receives FDA approval to sell Enovid as a birth control pill, which women's lives around the world and opens the door to the sexual revolution

1981 AIDS is discovered to be caused by the Human immunodeficiency virus (HIV). It is now a global pandemic.

1946 Center for Disease Control is founded as an evolution of Malaria Control in War Areas after World War II

1948 establishment of the World Health Organization [WHO]

1962 Rachel Carson raises awareness on pesticide use with her book Silent Spring, the Migrant Health Act was passed that same year

1970 The Nixon Administration establishes the Environmental Protection Agency

CDC

Examples of Complexity Thinking and Systems Theory
Globalization, *still* with a tacit understanding of medical geography

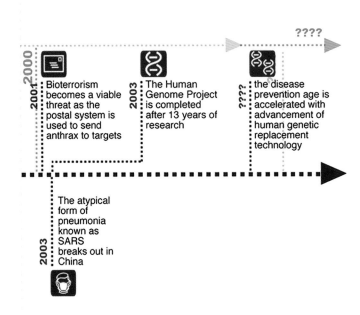

2000 **2001**: Bioterrorism becomes a viable threat as the postal system is used to send anthrax to targets

2003: The Human Genome Project is completed after 13 years of research

????: the disease prevention age is accelerated with advancement of human genetic replacement technology

2003: The atypical form of pneumonia known as SARS breaks out in China

Examples of Complexity Thinking and Systems Theory
19th century environmental determinism render borders a global threat

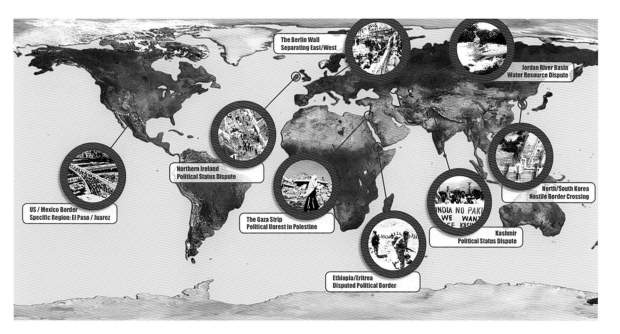

The Berlin Wall
Separating East/West

Jordan River Basin
Water Resource Dispute

Northern Ireland
Political Status Dispute

US / Mexico Border
Specific Region: El Paso / Juarez

The Gaza Strip
Political Unrest in Palestine

North/South Korea
Hostile Border Crossing

INDIA NO PAKI
WE WANT
CE KASH

Kashmir
Political Status Dispute

Ethiopia/Eritrea
Disputed Political Border

A form of xenophobic environmental determinism where beliefs, values, approaches toward conflict, resources, collective behavior developed at the center represent cultural difference embodied in designed institutions

An Important Paradigm Shift
To Distinguish Geopolitical Phenomena Under Dynamic Conditions

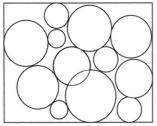

Policy formation as a function of intact geopolitical bodies does not recognize mobility, epidemics and shared disasters

An Important Paradigm Shift
To Distinguish Geopolitical Phenomena Under Dynamic Conditions

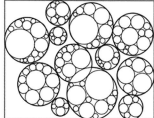

Compounded by scales of institutional and network influence

An Important Paradigm Shift
To Distinguish Geopolitical Phenomena Under Dynamic Conditions

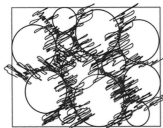

Policy design framework that recognizes dynamic conditions of geopolitical and natural systems integration

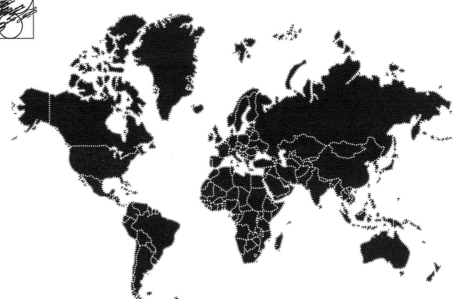

An Important Paradigm Shift
To Distinguish Geopolitical Phenomena Under Dynamic Conditions

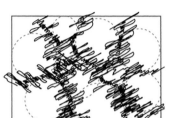

For a healthier health commons, we seek to develop a foundational analysis to begin to understand a shifting paradigm in global disease management more characteristic of a world of porous borders

U.S.- Mexico Border

Characterizing the Border
Migration and Integration

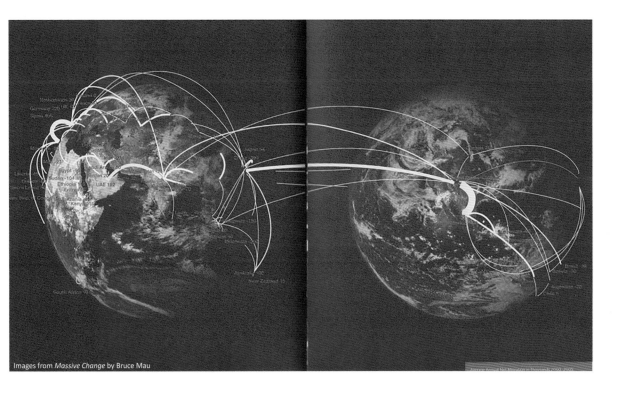

Images from *Massive Change* by Bruce Mau

Characterizing the Border
Migration and Integration

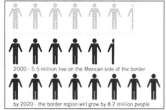

1 Population of the border region (each figure represents one million people)

2 Unauthorized, Mexican immigrants constitute a fair portion of multiple occupations in the US

3 The border's sister cities economies, environment, and health commons are entwined

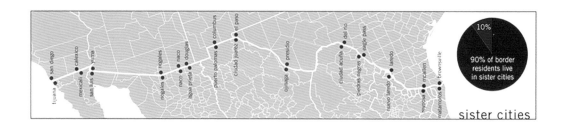

Statistics from "Hyperborder: The Contemporary US-Mexico Border and its Future" by Fernando Romero/LAR

U.S.- Mexico Border Health Commission
Health Disparities and the U.S.-Mexico Border: Challenges and Opportunities
Oct 25, 2010

Border challenges contribute to diminished health, well-being, and access to health care.

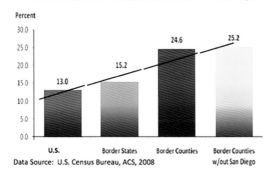

Persons Living below Poverty Level in the U.S. and Border Region

Data Source: U.S. Census Bureau, ACS, 2008

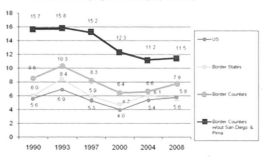

1990-2008 Unemployment Rate (in percents)

Source: Local Area Unemployment Statistics, U.S. Bureau of Labor Statistics

U.S.- Mexico Border Health Commission
Health Disparities and the U.S.-Mexico Border: Challenges and Opportunities
Oct 25, 2010

The border population poses challenges to the U.S. health care system: It is one of the fastest growing in the nation with a majority Hispanic population.

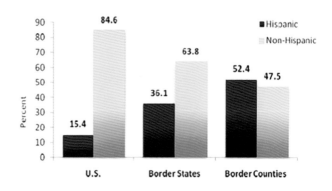

Data Source: Population Estimates, U.S. Census Bureau

U.S.- Mexico Border Health Commission
Health Disparities and the U.S.-Mexico Border: Challenges and Opportunities
Oct 25, 2010

Lack of health coverage in the border region has adverse consequences for health and health care.

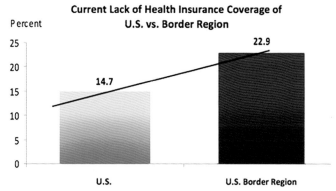

Current Lack of Health Insurance Coverage of
U.S. vs. Border Region

Data Source: 2000-2003, National Health Interview Survey, In-house data file, CDC/NCHS; Retrieved by Notzon, F. & Albertorio-Diaz, J.

U.S.- Mexico Border Health Commission
Health Disparities and the U.S.-Mexico Border: Challenges and Opportunities
Oct 25, 2010

U.S. residents often head south of the border due to the high cost of health care.

A study conducted in Texas border counties found that among those under age 65 who reported no health insurance were 3 to 7 times more likely to use medical care in Mexico than the insured.

41% of Hispanic residents in Laredo, TX use health services from Mexico.

86% of low-income residents in El Paso, TX use health services from Mexico.

37% of uninsured residents in New Mexico use health services from Mexico.

U.S.- Mexico Border Health Commission
Health Disparities and the U.S.-Mexico Border: Challenges and Opportunities
Oct 25, 2010

Border hospitals, health care providers, and community health centers continue to absorb growing uncompensated health care costs.

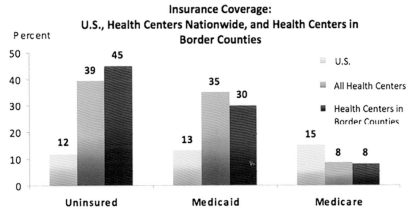

Data Source: National Association of Community Health Centers, Uniform Data System, 2007; Retrieved by M. Proser

U.S.- Mexico Border Health Commission
Health Disparities and the U.S.-Mexico Border: Challenges and Opportunities
Oct 25, 2010

The border region can serve as a source for identifying innovative models for reimagining global conditions orchestrated by shared formal and informal institutions.

These models bring together multiple levels of government and community leaders across geographic and jurisdictional borders by:

Improving access to health care at the fringe.

Creating a culture of wellness and prevention and strengthening the public health infrastructure for a healthy health commons.

Promoting evidence-based interventions and models of excellence.

... all of which can ensure deliberate and sustained actions to improve health conditions and thereby elevate the health of the nation.

Characterizing the Border
Systems Dynamics and Complex Feedbacks

Our approach: innovative models and next steps

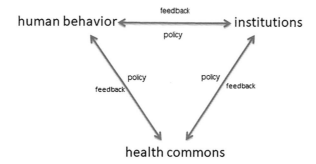

Characterizing the Border
Institutional Coordination and Individual Investment

$$\frac{dS}{dt} = -\sigma(\bar{c}_s, c_t)\lambda S + \gamma I$$

$$\frac{dI}{dt} = \sigma(\bar{c}_s, c_t)\lambda S - \gamma I$$

$$\lambda = \beta\frac{I}{N}, \quad N = S + I$$

$$U(c_s; \bar{c}_s, c_t) = \frac{u - c_t}{h} - \frac{(h+\gamma)c_s + \lambda^*\sigma(c_s, c_t)c_i}{h[h + \gamma + \lambda^*\sigma(c_s, c_t)]}$$

$$\frac{\partial \mathcal{U}}{\partial c_t}\Delta c_t > 0, \quad \text{but} \quad \left(\frac{\partial \mathcal{U}}{\partial c_s} + \frac{\partial \mathcal{U}}{\partial \bar{c}_s}\right)\frac{\partial c_s^*}{\partial c_t}\Delta c_t < 0.$$

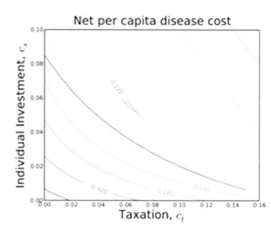

Net per capita disease cost

Individual Investment, c_s — Taxation, c_t

Characterizing the Border
Influence of institutional networks in behavior change

A network generated from formal participation in the 2007 meetings of four U.S.-Mexico agencies working on border health: the U.S.-Mexico Border Health Commission (USMBHC), U.S.-Mexico Border Health Association (UMSBHA), U.S.-Mexico Border Counties Coalition (USMBCC), and the Border Legislative Conference (BLC). The hubs represent the meetings; the ties represent participation in the meeting; the red circles represent U.S. agencies; blue triangles represent Mexican agencies; and black squares represent bi-national or multi-national agencies.

Network of participation in border health meetings in 2007

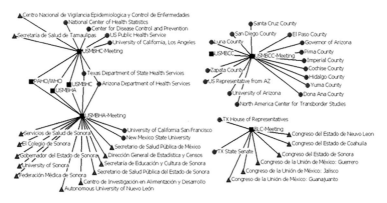

mapping successes and failures

Next steps | Determining what organizations are successes or failures
Study | Map the organizations with regard to how they approach the issues at
hand (is it top-down or bottom-up)-- if they are able to overcome the issues
associated with their particular approach and create a consistent chain of
information, they are a success

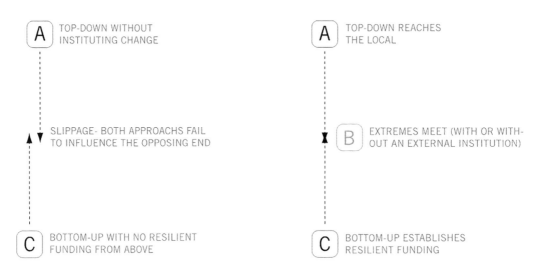

(A) TOP-DOWN WITHOUT
    INSTITUTING CHANGE

(A) TOP-DOWN REACHES
    THE LOCAL

SLIPPAGE- BOTH APPROACHS FAIL
TO INFLUENCE THE OPPOSING END

(B) EXTREMES MEET (WITH OR WITH-
    OUT AN EXTERNAL INSTITUTION)

(C) BOTTOM-UP WITH NO RESILIENT
    FUNDING FROM ABOVE

(C) BOTTOM-UP ESTABLISHES
    RESILIENT FUNDING

SUCCESS or failure - conclusions

grassroots:

fundamental; of or involving the common people as
constituting a fundamental political and economic group

http://wordnetweb.princeton.edu/perl/webwn?s=grassroots

who's working at the border

1) FEDERAL: Health Resources and Services Administration, Environmental Protection Agency, National Center for Farmworker Health, Farmworker Justice, Migrant Clinicians Network, National Head Start Association
2) STATE: California-Mexico Health Initiative
3) GRASSROOTS: Migrant/Seasonal Head Start, Campesinos Sin Fronteras, FEMAP/SADEC, Environmental Health Coalition

SUCCESS or failure

health resources and services administration (hrsa)

- Works to "improve access to health care services for people who are uninsured, isolated or medically vulnerable" (migrant/seasonal workers are considered under "medically vulnerable")
- Funds migrant health clinics, which, they estimate, serve 865,000 migrants a year
- Runs the National Advisory Council on Migrant Health (NACMH) which makes recommendations to the HHS concerning migrant worker health needs

SUCCESS or failure - federal

http://www.hrsa.gov; http://bphc.hrsa.gov/about/specialpopulations.htm

epa border 2012

- A collaborative effort between the US EPA and Mexican SEMARNAT to approach environmental issues along the border as a regional issue
- Through our research, we have determined that this project does not truly address regional issues, but instead focuses on discrete instances of environmental degradation

SUCCESS or failure - federal
http://www.epa.gov/Border2012/

national center for farmworker health

- A private, non-profit center working to better the health of migrant workers by providing them with health information and providing supplies to migrant health clinics
- Their website provides information about the demographics of US farmworkers and has a migrant health clinic directory
- Various educational programs focus on: asthma awareness, HIV/AIDS awareness, farmworker safety, cervical and breast cancer awareness, and more

SUCCESS or failure - federal

http://www.ncfh.org/

farmworker justice

- A non-profit organization located in Washington DC that advocates for farmworkers' rights
- Analyzes decisions made by the federal and state governments and protects the rights of works
- Little is said about the actual impact they have made or what discriminatory laws and regulations they have successfully overturned
- Poder Sano | A toolkit that assists promatoras in disseminating information concerning AIDS among migrant populations

FARMWORKER JUSTICE

SUCCESS or failure - federal

http://www.farmworkerjustice.org/

migrant clinicians network

- A non-profit national organization that brings together clinicians working in migrant health clinics, it currently has over 5,000 members
- The website contains a migrant health clinic directory for locating clinics anywhere in the nation
- Provides information unique to clinicians assisting migrant workers

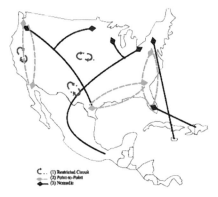

Darla V. Lindberg

SUCCESS or failure - federal

http://www.migrantclinician.org/about.html

national head start association (nhsa)

- A private, not-for-profit association dedicated to school readiness
- The NHSA is the advocacy group that allows the thousands of Head Starts across the country have a unified presence
- Go Smart I A program promoting healthy lifestyles by encouraging exercise in preschool aged children

SUCCESS or failure - federal

http://www.nhsa.org/; http://www.nhsa.org/services/programs/go_smart

california - mexico health initiative

- Initiative within the School of Public Health at UC Berkeley
- The initiative has created several health "stations" and runs several bilingual campaigns to assist migrants in finding adequate healthcare and information
- Piloted the idea of binational health insurance to allow migrants to receive medical care regardless of which country they reside

SUCCESS or failure - state

http://hia.berkeley.edu/

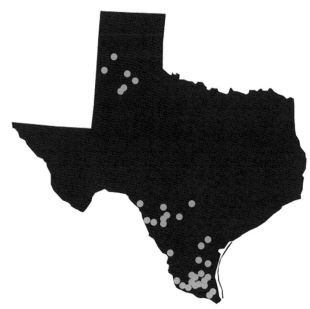

migrant/seasonal head starts - texas

- 54 of the hundreds of Texas Head Starts are migrant/seasonal head starts, all are run by the Texas Migrant Council, Inc
- None have websites, must be called to contact

SUCCESS or failure - grassroot

http://eclkc.ohs.acf.hhs.gov/hslc/HeadStartOffices

campesinos sin fronteras

- Works in Yuma County, AZ aiding migrant farm
  workers in three areas: housing, health, and
  education
- Runs numerous programs relating to health, two
  of interest are:
    - Diabetes Management Program (CDMP):
      A promotora-based diabetes management
      group that provides support and education
      for those with diabetes
    - Familias Sanas: A program that seeks,
      through education, to prevent chronic
      diseases, such as: cardiovascular disease,
      diabetes, and childhood obesity

SUCCESS or failure - grassroot

http://www.campesinossinfronteras.org/csfAbout.html

femap foundation

- The FEMAP Foundation is a US-based public charity – SADEC is a private, non-profit Mexican institution
- Works throughout the El Paso/Ciudad Juarez region, mainly with FEMAP-SADEC in relation to two hospitals and two promotora programs
- Supports promotora programs in the region:

    - Salud y Desarrollo Comunitario (SADEC) runs a promotora program in Ciudad Juarez

    - FEMAP's women-run promotora program in Juarez's colonias focuses on reproductive health issues and providing health care throughout the colonias

SUCCESS or failure - grassroot

http://www.femap.org/about_projects.sstg

environmental health coalition

- Works in the San Diego/Tijuana area
- Focuses on the environmental and public health issues that stem from the inappropriate use of toxic materials and pollution
- Works with other local grassroots organizations to pressure local and national organizations to clean up toxic sites and reduce the health issues related to these sites
    - Involved in the official dedication of 2200 acres of coastal wetlands for the South San Diego Bay National Wildlife Refuge
    - After five years, pressured the local government into enacting a policy against the use of the pesticide methyl bromide in nearby poor Latino communities, the first of its kind in the country
    - Helped the City of San Diego win an EPA "Emerging Brownfield" grant, the first of its kind

SUCCESS or failure - grassroot

http://www.environmentalhealth.org/About_EHC/index.html

Mapping Institutions
The Environmental Protection Agency

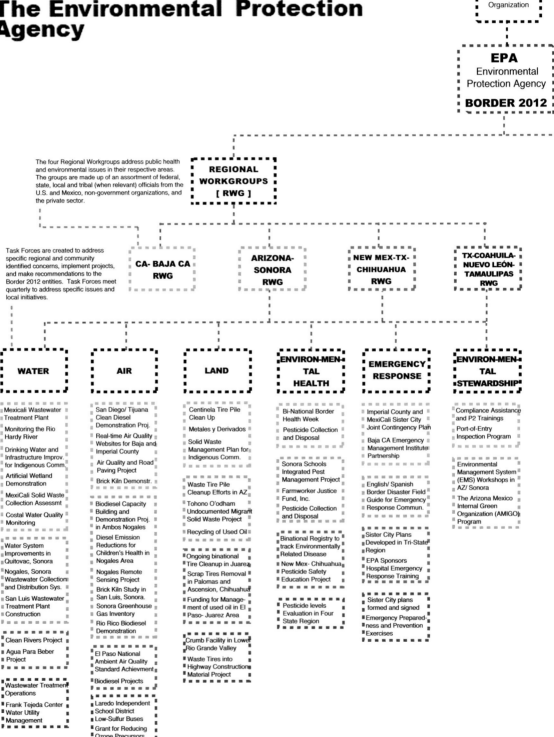

WHO
World Health Organization

EPA
Environmental Protection Agency
BORDER 2012

The four Regional Workgroups address public health and environmental issues in their respective areas. The groups are made up of an assortment of federal, state, local and tribal (when relevant) officials from the U.S. and Mexico, non-government organizations, and the private sector.

REGIONAL WORKGROUPS [RWG]

Task Forces are created to address specific regional and community identified concerns, implement projects, and make recommendations to the Border 2012 entities. Task Forces meet quarterly to address specific issues and local initiatives.

CA- BAJA CA RWG

ARIZONA-SONORA RWG

NEW MEX-TX-CHIHUAHUA RWG

TX-COAHUILA-NUEVO LEÓN-TAMAULIPAS RWG

WATER	AIR	LAND	ENVIRON-MEN-TAL HEALTH	EMERGENCY RESPONSE	ENVIRON-MEN-TAL STEWARDSHIP
Mexicali Wastewater Treatment Plant	San Diego/ Tijuana Clean Diesel Demonstration Proj.	Centinela Tire Pile Clean Up	Bi-National Border Health Week	Imperial County and MexiCali Sister City Joint Contingency Plan	Compliance Assistance and P2 Trainings
Monitoring the Rio Hardy River	Real-time Air Quality Websites for Baja and Imperial County	Metales y Derivados	Pesticide Collection and Disposal	Baja CA Emergency Management Institute Partnership	Port-of-Entry Inspection Program
Drinking Water and Infrastructure Improv. for Indigenous Comm.	Air Quality and Road Paving Project	Solid Waste Management Plan for Indigenous Comm.			
Artificial Wetland Demonstration	Brick Kiln Demonstr.		Sonora Schools Integrated Pest Management Project	English/ Spanish Border Disaster Field Guide for Emergency Response Commun.	Environmental Management System (EMS) Workshops in AZ/ Sonora
MexiCali Solid Waste Collection Assessmt	Biodiesel Capacity Building and Demonstration Proj. in Ambos Nogales	Waste Tire Pile Cleanup Efforts in AZ	Farmworker Justice Fund, Inc.		The Arizona Mexico Internal Green Organization (AMIGO) Program
Costal Water Quality Monitoring	Diesel Emission Reductions for Children's Health in Nogales Area	Tohono O'odham Undocumented Migrant Solid Waste Project	Pesticide Collection and Disposal		
Water System Improvements in Quitovac, Sonora	Nogales Remote Sensing Project	Recycling of Used Oil	Binational Registry to track Environmentally Related Disease	Sister City Plans Developed in Tri-State Region	
Nogales, Sonora Wastewater Collection and Distribution Sys.	Brick Kiln Study in San Luis, Sonora.	Ongoing binational Tire Cleanup in Juarez	New Mex- Chihuahua Pesticide Safety Education Project	EPA Sponsors Hospital Emergency Response Training	
San Luis Wastewater Treatment Plant Construction	Sonora Greenhouse Gas Inventory	Scrap Tires Removal in Palomas and Ascension, Chihuahua			
	Rio Rico Biodiesel Demonstration	Funding for Manage-ment of used oil in El Paso- Juarez Area	Pesticide levels Evaluation in Four State Region	Sister City plans formed and signed	
Clean Rivers Project				Emergency Prepared-ness and Prevention Exercises	
Agua Para Beber Project	El Paso National Ambient Air Quality Standard Achievment	Crumb Facility in Lower Rio Grande Valley			
Wastewater Treatment Operations	Biodiesel Projects	Waste Tires into Highway Construction Material Project			
Frank Tejeda Center Water Utility Management	Laredo Independent School District Low-Sulfur Buses				
	Grant for Reducing Ozone Precursors				

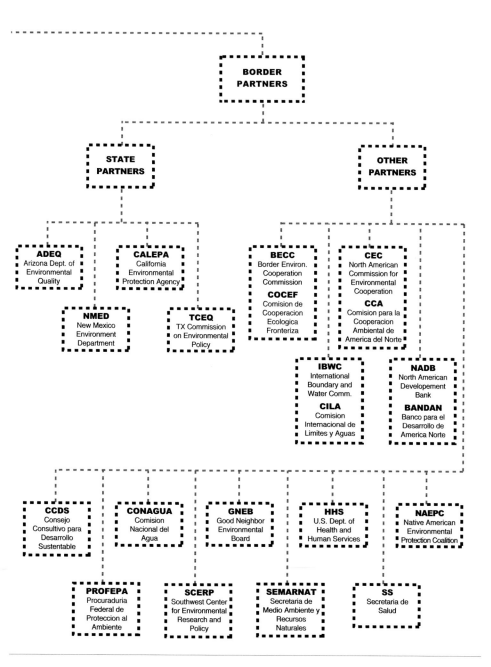

U.S.-Mexico Border Environmental and Health programs
1983-2002

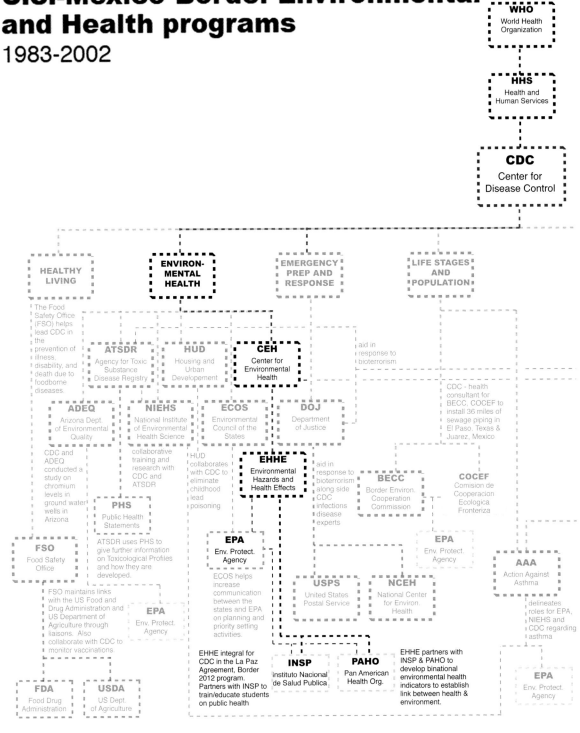

WHO
World Health Organization

HHS
Health and Human Services

CDC
Center for Disease Control

HEALTHY LIVING

ENVIRON-MENTAL HEALTH

EMERGENCY PREP AND RESPONSE

LIFE STAGES AND POPULATION

The Food Safety Office (FSO) helps lead CDC in the prevention of illness, disability, and death due to foodborne diseases.

ATSDR
Agency for Toxic Substance Disease Registry

HUD
Housing and Urban Developement

CEH
Center for Environmental Health

aid in response to bioterrorism

CDC - health consultant for BECC, COCEF to install 36 miles of sewage piping in El Paso, Texas & Juarez, Mexico

ADEQ
Arizona Dept. of Environmental Quality

NIEHS
National Institute of Environmental Health Science

ECOS
Environmental Council of the States

DOJ
Department of Justice

CDC and ADEQ conducted a study on chromium levels in ground water wells in Arizona

collaborative training and research with CDC and ATSDR

HUD collaborates with CDC to eliminate childhood lead poisoning

EHHE
Environmental Hazards and Health Effects

aid in response to bioterrorism along side CDC infections disease experts

BECC
Border Environ. Cooperation Commission

COCEF
Comision de Cooperacion Ecologica Fronteriza

PHS
Public Health Statements

ATSDR uses PHS to give further information on Toxicological Profiles and how they are developed.

EPA
Env. Protect. Agency

ECOS helps increase communication between the states and EPA on planning and priority setting activities.

EPA
Env. Protect. Agency

AAA
Action Against Asthma

FSO
Food Safety Office

USPS
United States Postal Service

NCEH
National Center for Environ. Health

delineates roles for EPA, NIEHS and CDC regarding asthma

FSO maintains links with the US Food and Drug Administration and US Department of Agriculture through liaisons. Also collaborate with CDC to monitor vaccinations.

EPA
Env. Protect. Agency

EHHE integral for CDC in the La Paz Agreement, Border 2012 program. Partners with INSP to train/educate students on public health

INSP
Instituto Nacional de Salud Publica

PAHO
Pan American Health Org.

EHHE partners with INSP & PAHO to develop binational environmental health indicators to establish link between health & environment.

EPA
Env. Protect. Agency

FDA
Food Drug Administration

USDA
US Dept. of Agriculture

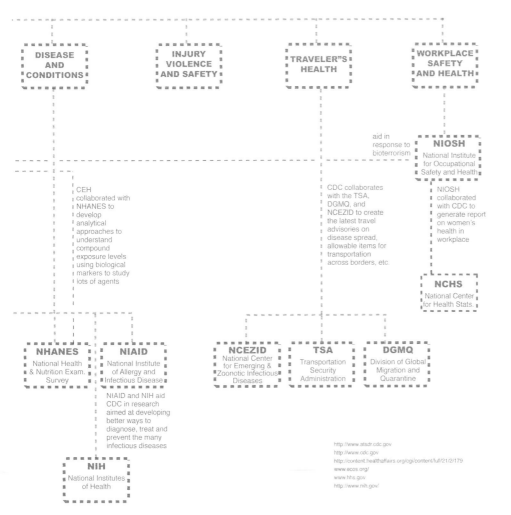

DISEASE AND CONDITIONS

INJURY VIOLENCE AND SAFETY

TRAVELER'S HEALTH

WORKPLACE SAFETY AND HEALTH

aid in response to bioterrorism

NIOSH
National Institute for Occupational Safety and Health

CEH collaborated with NHANES to develop analytical approaches to understand compound exposure levels using biological markers to study lots of agents

CDC collaborates with the TSA, DGMQ, and NCEZID to create the latest travel advisories on disease spread, allowable items for transportation across borders, etc.

NIOSH collaborated with CDC to generate report on women's health in workplace

NCHS
National Center for Health Stats.

NHANES
National Health & Nutrition Exam. Survey

NIAID
National Institute of Allergy and Infectious Disease

NCEZID
National Center for Emerging & Zoonotic Infectious Diseases

TSA
Transportation Security Administration

DGMQ
Division of Global Migration and Quarantine

NIAID and NIH aid CDC in research aimed at developing better ways to diagnose, treat and prevent the many infectious diseases

NIH
National Institutes of Health

http://www.atsdr.cdc.gov
http://www.cdc.gov
http://content.healthaffairs.org/cgi/content/full/21/2/179
www.ecos.org/
www.hhs.gov
http://www.nih.gov/

Mapping Institutions
The Center for Disease Control

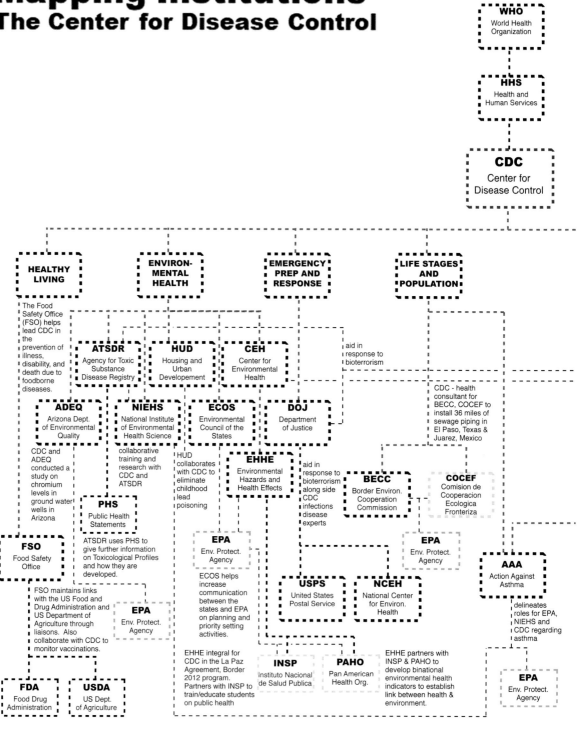

WHO — World Health Organization

HHS — Health and Human Services

CDC — Center for Disease Control

HEALTHY LIVING

The Food Safety Office (FSO) helps lead CDC in the prevention of illness, disability, and death due to foodborne diseases.

ENVIRON-MENTAL HEALTH

EMERGENCY PREP AND RESPONSE

LIFE STAGES AND POPULATION

ATSDR — Agency for Toxic Substance Disease Registry

HUD — Housing and Urban Developement

CEH — Center for Environmental Health

aid in response to bioterrorism

CDC - health consultant for BECC, COCEF to install 36 miles of sewage piping in El Paso, Texas & Juarez, Mexico

ADEQ — Arizona Dept. of Environmental Quality

NIEHS — National Institute of Environmental Health Science

ECOS — Environmental Council of the States

DOJ — Department of Justice

CDC and ADEQ conducted a study on chromium levels in ground water wells in Arizona

collaborative training and research with CDC and ATSDR

HUD collaborates with CDC to eliminate childhood lead poisoning

EHHE — Environmental Hazards and Health Effects

aid in response to bioterrorism along side CDC infections disease experts

BECC — Border Environ. Cooperation Commission

COCEF — Comision de Cooperacion Ecologica Fronteriza

PHS — Public Health Statements

ATSDR uses PHS to give further information on Toxicological Profiles and how they are developed.

EPA — Env. Protect. Agency

ECOS helps increase communication between the states and EPA on planning and priority setting activities.

EPA — Env. Protect. Agency

AAA — Action Against Asthma

FSO — Food Safety Office

FSO maintains links with the US Food and Drug Administration and US Department of Agriculture through liaisons. Also collaborate with CDC to monitor vaccinations.

EPA — Env. Protect. Agency

USPS — United States Postal Service

NCEH — National Center for Environ. Health

delineates roles for EPA, NIEHS and CDC regarding asthma

EHHE integral for CDC in the La Paz Agreement, Border 2012 program. Partners with INSP to train/educate students on public health

INSP — Instituto Nacional de Salud Publica

PAHO — Pan American Health Org.

EHHE partners with INSP & PAHO to develop binational environmental health indicators to establish link between health & environment.

EPA — Env. Protect. Agency

FDA — Food Drug Administration

USDA — US Dept. of Agriculture

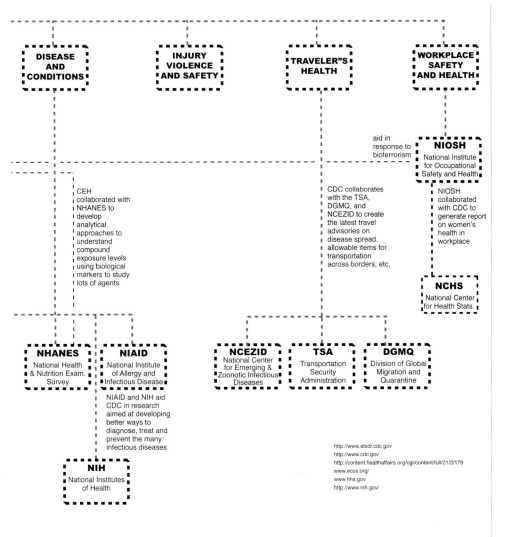

DISEASE
AND
CONDITIONS

INJURY
VIOLENCE
AND SAFETY

TRAVELER"S
HEALTH

WORKPLACE
SAFETY
AND HEALTH

aid in
response to
bioterrorism

NIOSH
National Institute
for Occupational
Safety and Health

CEH
collaborated with
NHANES to
develop
analytical
approaches to
understand
compound
exposure levels
using biological
markers to study
lots of agents

CDC collaborates
with the TSA,
DGMQ, and
NCEZID to create
the latest travel
advisories on
disease spread,
allowable items for
transportation
across borders, etc.

NIOSH
collaborated
with CDC to
generate report
on women's
health in
workplace

NCHS
National Center
for Health Stats.

NHANES
National Health
& Nutrition Exam.
Survey

NIAID
National Institute
of Allergy and
Infectious Disease

NCEZID
National Center
for Emerging &
Zoonotic Infectious
Diseases

TSA
Transportation
Security
Administration

DGMQ
Division of Global
Migration and
Quarantine

NIAID and NIH aid
CDC in research
aimed at developing
better ways to
diagnose, treat and
prevent the many
infectious diseases

NIH
National Institutes
of Health

http://www.atsdr.cdc.gov
http://www.cdc.gov
http://content.healthaffairs.org/cgi/content/full/21/2/179
www.ecos.org/
www.hhs.gov
http://www.nih.gov/

Policy Space

COLLECTIVE ACTION CONCEPTS AND STRATEGIES FOR INSTITUTIONAL DESIGN AND POLICY IMPLICATIONS WITH THE END GOAL OF RESILIENT COMMUNITY AND ECOLOGICAL DESIGN

POLICYSPACE

PROJECTS

RIO GRANDE VALLEY
TRANSIENT COMMUNITIES
INFECTIOUS DISEASE DYNAMICS
MORE INFORMATION TO BE UPLOADED

Conclusion

Therefore,
through this work we seek to develop a foundational analysis
to begin to understand a shifting paradigm in global disease management
more characteristic of a world of porous borders.

"We are in an era when the larger issues of public health intersect the practices of landscape architecture, architecture and urbanism. The causes of homegrown lifestyle diseases and of global pandemics are complex and interwoven; it will take many disciplines, working together, to devise solutions." ---Thomas Fischer, Dean, College of Design, University of Minnesota

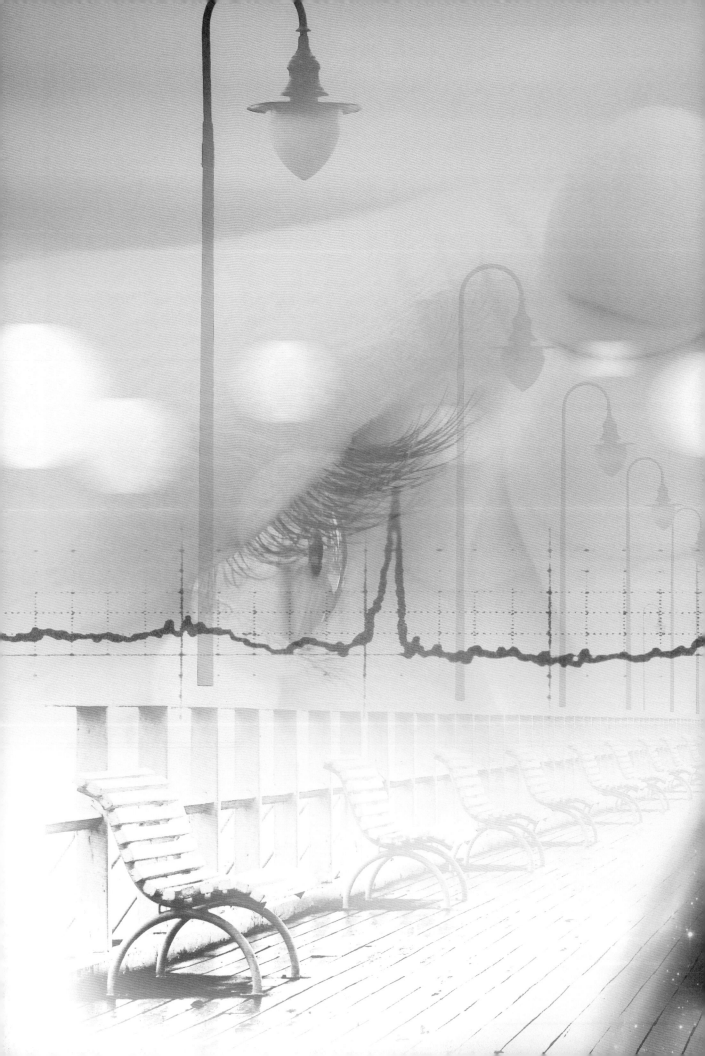

SYNCHRONICITY

The greatest status revolution

Carrying the legacy of possibly the greatest status revolutions in the history of the world, the Internet stands as a permanent reminder that technology is the expert equalizer. The 17th-century philosopher Gottfried Leibniz imagined the metaphysical *parallelism* of mind and matter because they cannot interact physically. Leibniz invented the binary system, the foundation of virtually all modern computer architectures.[93] According to Leibniz, mind and matter are supposed to exist in "pre-established harmony" like two synchronized clocks.[94] What Leibniz hadn't anticipated was the exploitation of advances such as the Internet to construct *asymmetrical information*. Stetson Kennedy did.[95] Asymmetrical information was coined by George Akerlof, co-winner of the 2001 Nobel Prize in Economics for his work investigating the causes of market malfunctions when buyers and sellers operate from different information.[96] His 1970 work *The Market for Lemons* established how markets—as in "lemon" used car markets—gave rise to the Lemon Law and spurred the development of behavioral economics as a burgeoning new field of study. Kennedy understood the power of asymmetrical information and used the *Superman* television show to turn the secrets of the Klu Klux Klan against itself. After watching the family's maid—who had pretty much raised Stetson—get tied to a tree, beaten and raped by a gang of Klansmen for talking back to a white trolley driver who had short-changed her, Kennedy joined the Klan with the intention of fighting bigotry from the inside. By handing off passwords and secret handshakes to the writers of the *Superman* television show young children turned precious knowledge into ammunition for mockery marked by "frown power" to demystify bigotry.[97] Had the Internet been available to Kennedy, the leverage of information asymmetry would have been even greater. Orson Welles' famous radio show *War of the Worlds* is possibly the most famous example of asymmetrical information. The radio show relied on listeners of the time to Trust the radio for the delivery of credible information about the world around them. Therefore, when the broadcaster announced the arrival of aliens to planet Earth on October 30, 1938, the United States experienced immediate mass hysteria.[98] The genius of using a counterpoint through asymmetrical information has become a model for everything from military information against enemy troops to calming civilians back home. It's been used to prevent a run-on-the-bank in order to stabilize the stock market, and drive campaigns for behavior change, i.e., quitting smoking, eating healthy, using seat belts, stopping littering. "Information is the currency of the Internet," writes Levitt and Dubner in *Freakonomics*.[99] And the Internet is brilliant at shifting information from the hands of those who have it into the hands of those who do not. Information asymmetry also played a part in the success story behind biologist Rachel Carson's revolutionary work *Silent Spring*.[100] Written as a work of literature because no science journal would publish her research, it caught public attention and sentiment to launch the environmental movement. Carson's work continues to trouble organizations such as the World Health Organization who would call for a reintroduction of DDT to developing countries.[101]

Possibly one of the more disturbing examples of asymmetrical information is illustrated by the story of the Enron collapse in 2001. *Enron: the smartest guys in the room*, is the name of a documentary.[102] It's not about business or politics; it's a story about crime. The documentary tells how Enron became one of the largest corporations in the country with what was essentially a Ponzi scheme and in the last days looted the retirement funds of its employees to buy a little more time and destroyed the Stock Market. The most shameful was the widespread complicit behavior among all the bankers, all the accountants and all the government agencies supposedly there for checks and balances. No one questioned how this was possible or what was happening until a *Fortune* magazine writer asked an innocent question when Enron's quarterly statements didn't seem to add up—"How does Enron make its money?" The documentary is based on the best-selling book, *Enron: the smartest guys in the room*, co-written by Bethany McLean and Peter Elkind. Using documentary and video footage, the film highlights congressional hearing testimony and interviews with former Enron executive Mike Muckleroy and whistleblower Sherron Watkins.

There is a general impression that Enron was a good corporation that went bad. The movie argues, however, that it was a con game almost from the start. Top executives Kenneth Lay and Jeff Skilling regularly touted Enron was the "best" company in the world. At the time they made that claim, they knew the company was bankrupt and had been worthless for years. To keep its stock price climbing, Enron fabricated quarterly returns to meet the numbers. One accounting tactic was called "mark-to-market," which meant if Enron began a venture that *might* make $50 million 10 years from now, it could claim the $50 million as current income today. Phony offshore accounts and corporate shell companies were used to funnel debt keeping Enron's books looking profitable. We're shown a schematic diagramming the movement of debt to such Enron entities. Two of the companies are named "M. Smart" and "M. Yass." These "companies" were named with reckless hubris: One stood for "Maxwell Smart" and the other, "My ass." It's hard to say exactly what Enron bought and sold. The corporation created a market in energy, gambled in it and manipulated it. It moved on into other futures markets, even seriously considering "trading weather." The film shows the close friendship between Kenneth Lay and both Bush administrations with Lay influencing deregulation on energy at the government level. In hindsight, Enron was a corporation devoted to maintaining a high share price at any cost. The "Stag Hunt" culture insisted failure was not an option. In-house video shows Lay and Skilling assuring employees and shareholders of the company's health at a time when Skilling, in particular, was coming apart at the seams. Especially chilling is how he sells $200million of his own Enron stock toward the end while encouraging Enron employees to invest their 401K retirement plans in the company. Then he suddenly resigns. And Enron collapses. Televised being taken away in handcuffs, both Skilling and Lay faced prison time. The film also shows Enron deceptively and knowingly tampering with the power grid in California creating a phony energy crisis which devastated the California economy at the time. In reality, there was never a shortage of power in California. The floor traders just made it appear that way. From tape recordings of Enron floor traders we hear them asking plant managers at California electrical plants to "get a little creative" in shutting down plants for "repairs." Between 30 percent and 50 percent of California's energy industry was shut down by this single publicly traded corporation creating a public perception of massive shortages in electrical power impacting stock prices for electricity to soar higher by nine times making Enron massive amounts of money. We hear Enron traders laughing about "Grandma Millie," as real people were suffering in California because of the rolling blackouts. They cheer, "burn baby burn" as they watch fires destroy California, fanning the public's fear of a power shortage and causing the stock market price of electricity to skyrocket. In the end, 20,000 employees are fired, their pensions are gone and their stock worthless. The press made it out to be a California problem only which diverted the fact that everyone's retirement and economies around the world had been collaterally affected. The horrific 9/11 attack on the Twin Towers in NYC of the same year overshadowed the Enron story and public hearings. But the cost of Enron's hubris was incalculable, not only in lives and property lost during the power crisis, but in an entire state economy: The state of California sued for $6 billion in refunds for energy overcharges collected during the phony crisis. Yet the crisis, made possible because Enron's lobbyists and Lay himself lobbied for deregulation, is still being blamed on too much regulation. If ever a corporation needed more regulation and oversight, it was Enron. And, if there was ever a time that needed more systems awareness oversight, *it was the twenty years between 1980 and 2000.*

When I think about a *perturbance* like Enron that was so far-reaching, affecting so many areas where other bright and responsible people *should* have been paying attention—accountants, bankers, environmentalists, politicians, parents, Wall Street, Main Street—I have to wonder about a possible blind spot and why? I'm reminded of a scene in the 2003 Academy Award nominated film, *Seabiscuit*. In the film, jockey George Woolf rides up alongside his friend "Red" Pollard who is riding Seabiscuit (the horse). Red is recovering from a bad leg injury. Woolf briefly checks on his friend and then announces, "there's my hole!" Pollard, blind in one eye, did not see that break and it cost him the race.[103] So, thinking about the massive amounts of complicity across the board I decided to take a systems-wide look into the twenty-year milieu (1980-2000) leading up to Enron's rise and fall. I found some disturbing insights.

First, we need to back up even further to what I refer to as the *Twenty-Year Generational Clock*.[104] A new generation reinvents itself every twenty years. At least in the United States, children are encouraged to leave home after high school, head to college, and start their own life at age 20. This is a vulnerable age. Success now means competing with a much larger mix of young adults all seeking the same thing. Considering the formative effects of the twenty-year phases a person goes through, context becomes everything.

Life at 15. A study by the Kaiser Foundation looked into the amount of time children ages 8 to 18 spent in front of technology and screens. Over a thousand families kept extensive daily diaries. Conducted in 2010, that study reported an average of 7 hours 38 minutes a day with digital media.[105] When using multiple devices, they spend more than 10.5 hours a day with digital technologies. "Digital Natives,"[106] as this group is called, are less concerned with how to run the world as to how to fit in to it. They may have opinions and struggle with the challenges of navigating in the world, but those values and views will play out in twenty to forty years *after* they grasp the mechanisms and take a leadership position.

The next twenty years of a human's life (15-35) are generally spent getting an education, building a family, buying a house, establishing a career. According to a report titled the "Four-Year Myth" from Complete College America, a nonprofit group based in Indianapolis, only 19 percent of full-time students in most public universities earn a bachelor's degree in four years.[107] Nationwide, only 50 of more than 580 public four-year institutions graduate a majority of their full-time students on time. Compounding those efforts, while people are taking longer to complete their education during this 20-year span, they are also, on average, more likely to start a family. According to a U.S. Census Bureau report, data since 1970 shows the median age for women marrying increased by 4.3 years to 25.1 and for men the increase was 3.6 years to 26.8 years. If having children is in the picture, even with medical advances, getting pregnant past 35 becomes challenging. In other words, people are still more likely to marry and start a family before age 35.[108] As if that isn't enough, a 2009 American Housing Data Survey and a 2012 report by the National Association of Realtors cites the average age for first time home buyers is between 31 and 34. After college graduation, graduate school, or an entry level job, people are able to pay off student loans and find their groove around 26 and 27. In other words, a lot is going on in the 20 years from 15-35. It's no surprise, for while there are always exceptions, this age group is the least likely to run for office or take on leadership roles in their neighborhood or company.

A financial blog by Alvarez and Marshal report the average age of a CEO, CFO, and COO is 52-56.[109] And, while mandatory retirement is extended out to 75 for many companies, the average age for presidents, VPs, directors, and managers in leadership positions still typically falls between 35 and 55. This is the twenty-year span where most of the decision making and leadership affecting policy and direction take place. Even constitutional eligibility to run for the Presidency of the United States is after the age of 34.[110] Anyone older than 55 is generally concerned with the next chapter – retirement, or dealing with aging parents, or supporting adult children, grandchildren, or as people are living longer, even starting new families themselves. And those older than 75 are dealing with health issues, aging issues, or enjoying their families and friends in retirement. In other words, while we all know exceptions to these statistics, those between 35 to 55 are the key decision makers in most positions of power for any generation. Overlaying this influential age group with key economic and political cycles throughout history tells a fascinating story of generational clocks.

Back to the blind spot leading up to Enron. The twenty years marking the end of the 1900s included a defining mix of unprecedented high interest rates (18-19%), high unemployment (10%), Keynesian economics after WWII to help with the recession in the '70s, a swing to conservatism in reaction to the tightening of money, and unprecedented wealth by folks capitalizing on energy and infrastructure after the early ages of the Industrial Revolution. The group now entering the influential 35-55 age zone are the Baby Boomers (first 1946 post-war babies + 35 = 1981). Anyone who fought in WWII was born to parents who had suffered through WWI setting up massive Trust issues within this generation at this age. Born in the wake of one World War, having survived the Great Depression and a second World War, they now lived in the shadow of the Cold War. So, the twenty years at the end of the millennium could be depicted as a perfect storm for corporate hubris, global demand for energy, market complicity, conservative mindset, and a longing for a knight in shining armor to bail us out of this malaise. More to the point, people had lost patience with government and regulation to solve the range of enormous problems engulfing the world at the time. Therefore, pushing government oversight out of the way and championing a wave of deregulation in every market, opened up the door for an arbitrage rampage by Wall Street and the case of the largest corporate fraud in the century. I share the story of Enron because any 15-35-year old coming into an age of leadership is probably not aware of it.

The *Theory of Cycles*—or forecast cycles—dates back to the 1800s.[111] Cycles, systems, and patterns capturing a milieu in climate, crop yield, cold summers, hot winters, economic highs and lows and cultural definers have been considered for over 200 years beginning as far back as 1810. Samuel Benner was a prosperous farmer who was wiped out by the 1873 panic and hog cholera epidemic.[112] When he retired, he studied the causes and timing of fluctuations in the economy. He charted an 11-year cycle in corn and pig prices with peaks alternating every five or six years. Cotton prices also moved in a 11-year cycle. Pig iron fell into a 27-year cycle with low prices hitting every eleven, nine and seven years and peaks every eight, nine and ten years. The original Benner Cycle Chart published in 1875 was used to predict U.S. crises or recessions well into the 20th century. Fluctuations seemed to indicate panics every 16, 18, 20 years repeating every 54 years. Benner's charts indicated "it takes panics 54 years in their order to make a revolution or to return to the same order."[113] A. J. Frost adapted the Benner Cycle to financial times and saw the 54-year cycle strongly linked to financial trends since the 1903-04 Crisis—the Dow Jones Industrial Average (DJIA) Bear Market Low.[114] Other events in the chart are the 1920-21 Panic (1903+18 = 1921), WWII (1921+20=1941), Recession (1941+16=1957), Crisis (1957+18=1975). The only event that doesn't correspond is there was no major low in 1995 (1975+20=1995). Part of the explanation is the Federal Reserve's dropping of the gold standard in 1971 which allowed the government to pump money into the system to help mediate and stimulate dropping markets. Similar cycles can be seen for 8-9-10-year cycles of DJIA market highs as well. Most notable are the 1929 market high and the 1929-33 Great Depression. These dates aligned with major market turns or financial panics and natural disasters. The Rio Grande River, for example, has a "well-known" 18-year flood cycle. Likewise, the center of every other continent—Africa, South

America, North America, and Asia—all have recorded an 18.6-year cycle of drought, floods, or other weather phenomena. Altogether, they also support the 56-year cycle, a key number in Cycle Theory. Where Cycle Theory hasn't been applied is with the influential age group—those 35-55—in positions of leadership and decision making at key point within these market cycles. My critique is directed here—towards history and it's inability to work with synchronous other histories to address the loss of institutional memory between one domain and another as it spans one generation to the next. History that biases only events and not systems cycles can lead to blind spots (recall "Red" Pollard) in systems awareness. This is not coincidence; this is pattern recognition. From John Nash to Arthur Samuel, mapping patterns, machine learning, and artificial intelligence have been used to forecast systems behaviors in the universe, statistics, epidemiology, engineering, and finance. Machine learning is used to devise complex models and algorithms that lend themselves to "produce reliable, repeatable, decisions and results" and uncover "hidden insights" through learning from historical relationships and trends in the data.[115]

Markets have been shown to move in patterns and cycles. The most prevalent cycle used in market forecasts is the 16-18-20-year cycle. However, the Twenty-Year Cycle, one phase of a single human life-cycle, happens too quickly for humans to absorb massive change. Massive change biases huge financial arbitrage opportunities by corporations and politicians utilizing the Trigger strategically in the societal version of the Stag Hunt. The Trigger works because it largely dismantles the work of the previous generation at the foundational level and lures the world into a Stag Hunt mentality striving for the next newest greatest thing (consider a charismatic new voice in politics catering to an impatient mindset—we saw it already in the 20 years leading up to Enron). The twenty-years between age 35 and 55, when a generation has the most opportunity for influence, is actually operating under impressions, biases and issues toward Trust reflected in the institutions and policies cast by those age 35-55 in the generation before it. We inherit the institutions designed by that generation. History would point to a predictable pendulum swing in the other direction by the next 35-55 age group.

Twenty-year Lag and Why It Matters
a whole systems observation of generational clocks

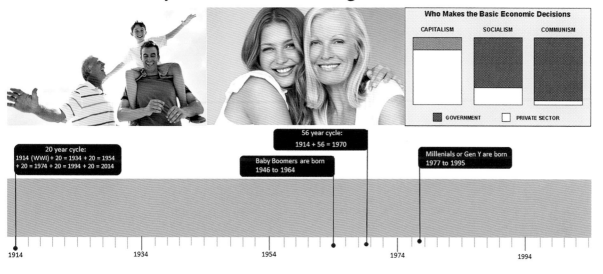

Who Makes the Basic Economic Decisions

CAPITALISM SOCIALISM COMMUNISM

GOVERNMENT PRIVATE SECTOR

20 year cycle:
1914 (WWI) + 20 = 1934 + 20 = 1954
+ 20 = 1974 + 20 = 1994 + 20 = 2014

56 year cycle:
1914 + 56 = 1970

Baby Boomers are born
1946 to 1964

Millenials or Gen Y are born
1977 to 1995

1914   1934   1954   1974   1994

A recent study reported on NPR presented Millennials' over-whelming preference for a socialist or communist society over their Baby Boomer parents' preference for a capitalist one. Re-searchers blamed a lack of knowledge of History. But not his-tory-as-Survey-of-the-Past as the Baby Boomer generation con-strued it. Instead, history as current phenomenon chronicled in the fine grain complexity of intermingling systems of economics, environmentalism, policy formation, and power filtered through the dynamic lens of social media. Leveraging Systems Theory principles—the whole-to-the-part—this presentation explores a macro-to-micro systems analysis of political, environmental and economic influences making perturbations such as the Enron Scandal of 2001 possible. Still considered the largest willful cor-porate scandal of the century, self-interest and hubris destroyed economies, ecologies, retirements, and lives. Looking back, Rea-ganomics and deregulation were logical, if not predictable, out-comes of a conservative generational pendulum swing. Today (2018), Jeff Skilling, CEO of Enron Corporation at the time of its fall, is released from prison. And just at a time when conserva-tive views are calling, again, for the deregulation of banks and the erosion of watchful environmental policy. The policy work done to safeguard us against incidents like Enron are viewed as excessive and unnecessary. Edmund Burke said, "those who don't know history are doomed to repeat it." But, those who can't identify the complexity circumstances distinguishing ar-bitrage opportunities from coincidence are just plain doomed. Perhaps it's time to develop tools to better understand this gen-erational twenty-year-lag as a function of a larger society's or-ganismal act of survival.

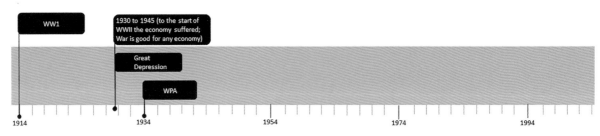

My dad, born 1914, was 16 years old during the Great Depression and was driving a truck to build roads for the Work Progress Administration (WPA), one of the relief programs President Franklin D. Roosevelt signed into action.

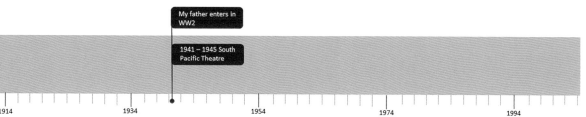

My father enters in
WW2

1941 – 1945 South
Pacific Theatre

1914   1934   1954   1974   1994

Then at age 28, now the only unmarried male in his family, he
was drafted to the Army at the start of WWII. As a hard-working farmer with an athletic build, he was sent to San Diego to
train in Jiu-jitsu martial arts and then deployed to fight in the
South Pacific. He survived four years on the front lines experiencing ground combat and three major invasions.

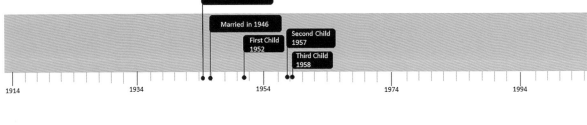

If you are keeping track of the time-line, it is now 1946. The War is over and the world is rebuilding and retooling every wartime advance into domestic progress. My parents met at a local dance and married that same year. Mom was 26, Dad was 32. She was one of the lucky ones. After WWII, 250,000 men never came home. For the first time in the United States, women outnumbered men.

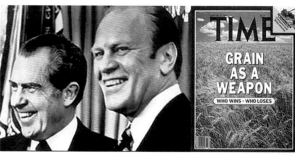

Unemployment rates over time
– Rise during contractions
– Fall during expansions
– The great Depression, 1930s, 25%
– Trended upward, mid-1940s to 1940s
– 1980s to 2000: Overall downward trend
  • A high 10% in 1982 to a low 4% in 2000
– Recession of 2001
  • 6% by 2003; declined into 2007

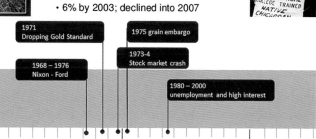

1971
Dropping Gold Standard

1975 grain embargo

1968 – 1976
Nixon - Ford

1973-4
Stock market crash

1980 – 2000
unemployment and high interest

| 1914 | 1934 | 1954 | 1974 | 1994 |

Twenty years later, between 1973 and 1975, the Western world suffered the greatest economic stagnation putting an end to the overall Post-World War II economic expansion. This was worse than previous recessions in that the country suffered high unemployment and high inflation. Hindsight pointed to the dropping of the gold standard in 1971, the oil crisis of 1973 and the stock market crash in 1973-74. The recession lasted through the Nixon presidency, the Ford presidency and, while there was a slight uptick in 1975, 10% unemployment and unprecedented 18-19% interested rates dominated the early 1980s.

Strauss-Howe Generational Definitions

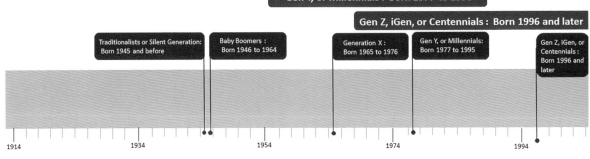

William Strauss and Neil Howe are generally credited for naming
the 20th century generations in their 1991 book, *Generations*.

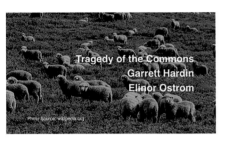

Trust and Self-Interest

Darla V. Lindberg

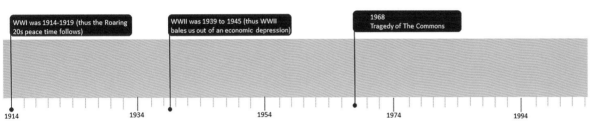

Trust—the fine grain complexity influence that takes a lifetime
to build and an instant to destroy.

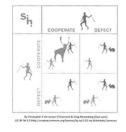

By Christopher R Jon Jensen (CXizeroom) & Greg Restenberg (Own work)
[CC BY-SA 3.0 (http://creativecommons.org/licenses/by-sa/3.0)] via Wikimedia Commons

The Stag Hunt and the Trigger

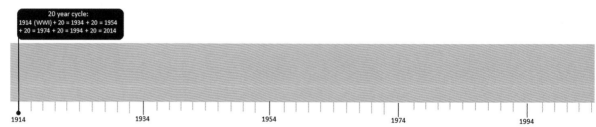

20 year cycle:
1914 (WWI) + 20 = 1934 + 20 = 1954
+ 20 = 1974 + 20 = 1994 + 20 = 2014

1914   1934   1954   1974   1994

Triggers are an essential tool in the Stag Hunt used to alter the status quo. If cooperation breaks down in the group and factions decide to splinter off and hunt hare, a strategic decision to switch and hunt stag can excite the group into trusting one another and cooperating for the greater outcome. Likewise, if the status quo has been risk dominant pressuring the group to take greater and greater chances, a "free-rider" can drop back and benefit from the efforts of the group without engaging in the risks of the hunt.

DNA of Leadership

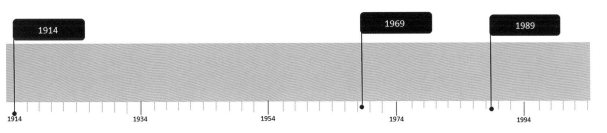

Considering the formative effects of the twenty-year phases a person goes through, context becomes everything.

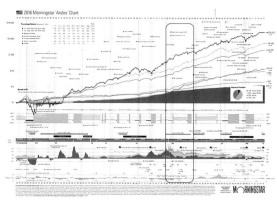

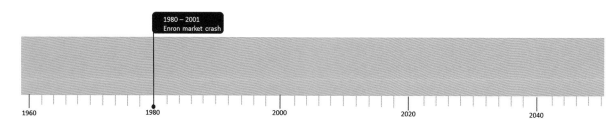

1980 – 2001
Enron market crash

1960   1980   2000   2020   2040

The twenty years at the end of the millennium could be depicted as a perfect storm of corporate hubris, global demand for
energy, market complicity, conservative mindset, and a longing for a knight in shining armor to bail us out of this malaise.
More to the point, people had lost patience with government
and regulation to solve the range of enormous problems engulfing the world at the time. Therefore, pushing government
oversight out of the way and championing a wave of deregulation in every market opened up the door for an arbitrage
rampage by Wall Street and the case of the largest corporate
fraud in the century.

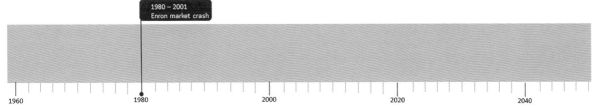

1980 – 2001
Enron market crash

1960   1980   2000   2020   2040

Enron: the smartest guys in the room, is the name of a documentary. It's not about business or politics; it's a story about crime. If there was ever a corporation that needed more regulation, that corporation was Enron. And, if there was ever a time that needed more systems awareness oversight, it was the twenty years between 1980 and 2000.

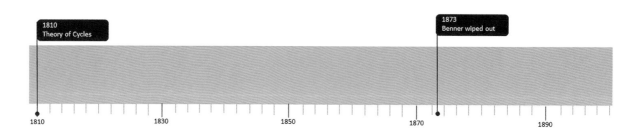

BENNER'S PROPHECIES

OF

FUTURE UPS AND DOWNS IN PRICES.

WHAT YEARS TO MAKE MONEY ON PIG-IRON, HOGS, CORN,
AND PROVISIONS.

By SAMUEL BENNER,
An Ohio Farmer.

"I know of no way of judging of the future but by the past."
—PATRICK HENRY.

DEDICATED

TO THE

AGRICULTURAL, MANUFACTURING, MINING, MERCANTILE,
INDUSTRIAL, FINANCIAL, AND COMMERCIAL INTER-
ESTS OF THE UNITED STATES OF AMERICA.

1810
Theory of Cycles

1873
Benner wiped out

1810   1830   1850   1870   1890

Samuel Benner was a prosperous farmer who was wiped out by
the 1873 panic and hog cholera epidemic. When he retired, he
studied the causes and timing of fluctuations in the economy.

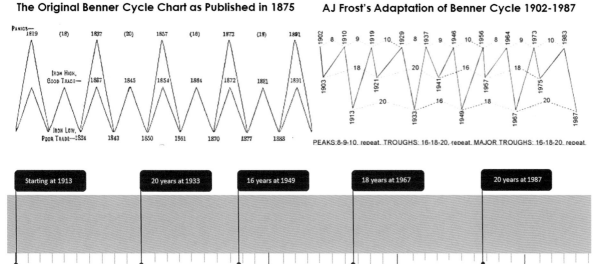

A. J. Frost adapted the Benner Cycle to financial times and saw the 54-year cycle strongly linked to financial trends since the 1903-04 Crisis.

Theory of Cycles – Forecast Cycles

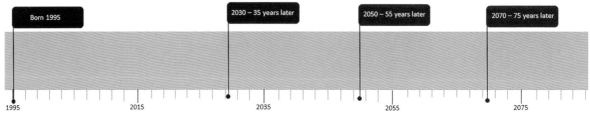

From John Nash to Arthur Samuel, mapping patterns, machine learning, and artificial intelligence have been used to forecast systems behaviors in the universe, statistics, epidemiology, engineering, and finance. Machine learning is used to devise complex models and algorithms that lend themselves to "produce reliable, repeatable, decisions and results" and uncover "hidden insights" through learning from historical relationships and trends in the data.

Systems Theory

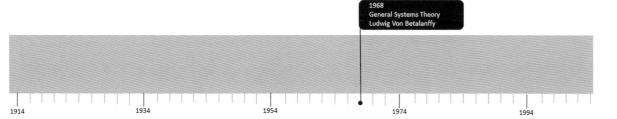

1968
General Systems Theory
Ludwig Von Betalanffy

1914   1934   1954   1974   1994

Investigating social theories and systems behaviors teaches us the biggest cultural perturbations are easier to absorb over time—the changing nature of family and life (health, welfare), the way Main Street works (currency, production), developing infrastructure for production and consumption.

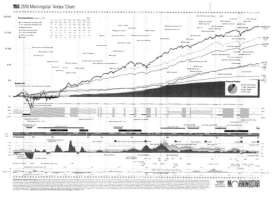

Big cultural changes are easier to absorb over time —

Nature of family and life - health, welfare

Main Street – currency, production

Developing Infrastructure – production, consumption

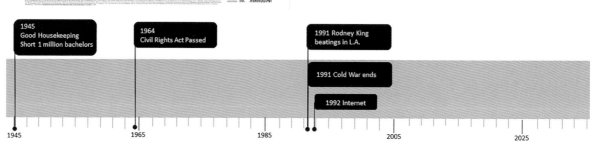

1945
Good Housekeeping
Short 1 million bachelors

1964
Civil Rights Act Passed

1991 Rodney King
beatings in L.A.

1991 Cold War ends

1992 Internet

1945   1965   1985   2005   2025

More and more, artists, designers and architects are moving beyond traditional fee-for-service to engage in complexity research and best practices influencing innovation, land-use development and resource management shaping our urban and non-urban places.

Design is a Coercive Act

2013
Detroit Bankruptcy July
18th

2016
Alejandro Aravena –
Pritzker Prize Winner

1973　　　1993　　　2013　　　2033　　　2053

Design is a coercive act. The 2016 Pritzker Prize awarded to Alejandro Aravena "triggered" a debate over whether work dedicated to improving the global housing crisis IS architecture. The people involved in the reimagining of Detroit are benefiting from the failed project of the industrial city—a low risk chance to try anything. Architects write the code—whether they do this by designing kick-ass places, deploying innovative materials, or they do this through visionary regulation and ethical-minded code. Either way, design changes the world.

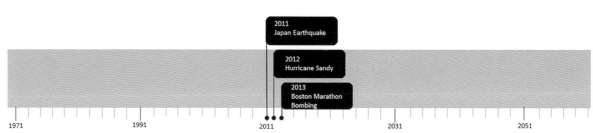

2011
Japan Earthquake

2012
Hurricane Sandy

2013
Boston Marathon
Bombing

1971   1991   2011   2031   2051

By addressing climate volatility and social movements in humanitarian rights (especially and including world-wide women's rights), the Twenty-Year Trigger becomes a powerful tool to shift us to a cooperative world designed to be in equilibrium and equity with the planet and with one another.

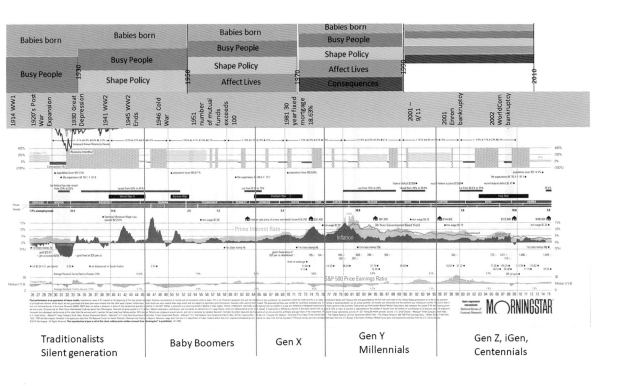

Mapping the Strauss-Howe Generations and the twenty-year phases of human development over key economic, political and cultural events around the world. Note in particular the twenty-year phases of influence and the twenty-year phases of leadership.

Twenty Year Key:

Babies Born 0 - 15 years of age

Busy People 15 - 35 years of age

Shape Policy 35 - 55 years of age

Affect Lives 55 - 75 years of age

Consequences 75 - 95 years of age

Moralist turned economist

Marcel Proust puzzled over the self-satisfaction felt by "busy men" at not having time to do what they needed to do.[116] Poets and musicians express the spectacular gaps in understanding created with the unexpected and hurtful behavior of another. Accountants and lovers might possibly agree the letter that needs to be written holds far more truth and affection than the letter that gets sent. De Botton wrote in his delightful *How Proust Can Change Your Life*, "Afraid of losing her, we forget all the others. Sure of keeping her, we compare her with those others whom at once we prefer to her."[117] Similarly, Adam Smith set out to be a moralist but became an economist instead.[118] Following the money to see how economic factors shaped the way a person thought or behaved it became apparent the incentives, the innocuous choice, and the friction between individual desire and societal norms were the more significant stuff of the modern moral life. In nature and society, systems of probability and indeterminacy are realistic. Many of life's most compelling puzzles are revealed to us through a synchronous other incident. Riddled with approximation, the near miss, the chance meeting, life unfolds as parallel events merge. Stochastic systems become even more realistic since they apply chance to the structure of probability. Entries can be added, changed or removed in a stochastic system creating mutations. A Markov Chain is a stochastic system, a transition.[119] While it takes longer for a condition of probability to achieve equilibrium and even a final result of stability is uncertain, over time the behavior of the system can be analyzed and predicted statistically (e.g., a coin toss has a 50% probability of being heads and a 50% chance of being tails). Markov Chains are a significant part of Game Theoretic analysis to consider choice and consequence. Metamorphosis is a stochastic mutation over time and influence. Larger systems increase variety and with it, probability. World economies, natural resources, population dynamics, disease spread and ecological relationships are complicated and intricate legacies of the "what if?" of probability and chance. De Certeau's observation that "The imaginary landscape of an inquiry is not without value, even if it is without rigor...(I)t thus keeps before our eyes the structure of a social imagination in which the problem constantly takes different forms and begins anew."[120]

$$X_{present\ state} + 1 = X_{next\ state}$$

Synchronous systems provide a critical framework for comprehending something as potentially overwhelming as neo-liberal economics research which when networked to agricultural production shows a high probability that the same industrial practices forcing tens of millions of farmers off the land by growing primarily high-profit exports also creates a production model for crop acreage that contributes to a loss of biodiversity in the natural systems ecologies and species—fundamentally our first line of defense in disease-spread threats.

My father was born in 1914 to first generation Swedish immigrant farmers settling in northern North Dakota. That meant when he was 16—a time when most men are learning to drive and generally making their parents crazy with concern—he was in the middle of the Great Depression. He had to quit school and drive a truck to build roads for the Work Progress Administration (WPA)- just one of the relief programs President Franklin D. Roosevelt signed into action.[121] At that formative age, he was exposed to learning some of the hardest lessons of survival. As a result, he kept his head down, developed a keen sense of watchfulness, helped his family through the hard times and started building his own grain farm in North Dakota. Then at age 28, now the only unmarried male in his family, he was drafted to the Army at the start of WWII. As a hard-working farmer with an athletic build, he was sent to San Diego to train in Jiu-jitsu martial arts and then deployed to fight on the front lines in the South Pacific. He experienced three major invasions over four years. Prior to leaving for the War he had been building his own grain farm in North Dakota. When he was drafted he sold his farm to his dad for a dollar with the handshake agreement that, should he return, he would buy it back. He did return and continued to build a fifteen hundred acre grain farm. The few stories he could share with us left unthinkable images of war—pregnant women with bayonets in their stomachs, buddies shot in fox-holes next to him. We filled in the blanks with the fact that he only had partial hearing in one ear and he couldn't go near fireworks on the 4th of July. He left for the war thinking he would never return and returned home a quiet reflective war hero to a ticker-tape-parade.

If you are keeping track of the timeline, it is now 1946. The War is over and the world is rebuilding and retooling every wartime advance into domestic progress. My parents met at a local dance and married that same year. Mom was 26, Dad was 32. She was one of the lucky ones. After WWII, 250,000 men never came home. For the first time in the United States, women outnumbered men. In June, 1945, *New York Times Magazine* predicted 750,000 women who wanted to marry would have to live alone.[122] *Good Housekeeping* captioned a photo of a bride and groom descending church steps with, "She got a man, but 6 to 8 million women won't. We're short 1 million bachelors."[123] The long-term effects of a shortage of men on institutions like marriage, family and the workforce as a result of global events like War had yet to be studied. But the clues were all there. Mom was among this group of women building her own Hope Chest—by the time she married she possessed her own dishes and linens, owned furs and furniture. She had an excellent job working for the Post Office living at home with her parents.

My parents were natural systems farmers before it was fashionable to be so. The farm was located across from a National Wildlife Refuge close to the Canadian border. Accounting notes from their large burgundy leather ledger kept track of Canadian geese migrating south and the thickness of animal hide. My dad would trap (and release) animals to get a sense of animals preparing their winter coat. When I moved to Pennsylvania I share boarded one season with the stables that hosted the Penn State Equestrian team. One fall we had a very hard, very early frost. I called the stable owner to check if the horses had "their hide?" He responded, "the smart ones did." Early or late frost, or hard frosts or mild winter, validated by animal hide, were a reliable indicator of the viability and robustness of weeds and pests for the following summer. Too much snow accumulation too late could delay sowing the seeds that spring and a golden crop ready for harvest in a late summer morning could be destroyed that afternoon with a ten-minute hailstorm. We learn intuitively the impact of *early frost and finance*. Spring that far north wasn't announced by the arrival of warming temperatures but by the appearance of saucers of damp dishcloths set along a south-facing window in the house folded over sprouting grain seeds predicting germination. Long before genetically modified grains and laws prohibiting farmers from using their own seeds, labels indicated grain storage bins to be used for sale or for planting another season. All fifteen hundred acres were never all in production at the same time. One-third would be planted with wheat, oats, flax or sunflowers; another third would consist of fields of alfalfa restoring rich nitrogen to the soil to be bailed and sold for hay to Montana ranchers; the other third would be summer fallow one growing season to turn the alfalfa back into the earth eliminating the need to use chemical fertilizers. Only once do I recall the sight of airplanes flying over our crops to spray for grasshoppers one tragic summer. And the summer before I went away for college we had a harvest so bountiful it resulted in dumping grain on tarps on the ground for transport later to Minneapolis for storage. Our own grain storage bins would not hold it all. My father and sister and I would ride horses each night to make the rounds to check on the crops. While my sister and I would enjoy hours of racing our horses around barrels set in the fields, my parents would walk deep into the fields checking the crops to determine the day of harvest. Harvest involved the entire community. Workers for hire and neighbors would arrive and work one farm after another. Neighbors provided the extra equipment and migrant workers provided the labor to keep the trucks and combines running all night should the night air allow it. Old photographs show men proudly lined up beside swathed rows of grain as wide as they were tall in front of a cascade of combines—one after another—disappearing in to the horizon. Since the land was so flat it was an impressive line-up.

My interest in studying Architecture and Landscape Architecture grew from that kind of respect for the synthesis of environment, equipment, weather, wildlife, chemistry, agronomy, economics, and community. When you *follow the money*, you see how the local bankers and implement dealers invested in the farmers' wisdom and going to church on Sunday was an act of faith—community orchestrated through a common labor pool for harvest or helping a neighbor in need.

They had three kids between 1952 and 1958. Their life story is not unique. Theirs is among the formative DNA of the '50s—the good 'ole days. They bought a new American car with cash every two years. Post-traumatic stress disorder played out in a never-tiring effort to make things right. With one paycheck a year at harvest time, and a perpetual fear of credit and spending, farmers implemented everything else they needed—raised their own beef, chickens, eggs, milk and gardens. Looking back, a compulsion to fix, ration, sew and preserve were as much post-war systemic symptoms of PTSD as they taught vigilance, frugality, faith, and wisdom—in other words, *always waiting for the other shoe to drop*.

And then it did. Twenty years later, between 1973 and 1975, the Western world suffered the greatest economic stagnation putting an end to the overall Post-World War II economic expansion.[124] This was worse than previous recessions in that the country suffered high unemployment and high inflation. Hindsight pointed to the dropping of the gold standard in 1971, the oil crisis of 1973 and the stock market crash in 1973-74.[125] The recession lasted through the Nixon presidency, the Ford presidency and, while there was a slight uptick in 1975, 10% unemployment and unprecedented 18-19% interested rates dominated the early 1980s.[126] I had just graduated from college and had been working for an architectural firm since the summer of my third year in Architecture. With interest rates at an all-time high, that meant money was expensive and building was limited to institutions who could afford it—banks, hospitals and government funded affordable housing. Architectural firms doing work at this time expressed this economy of means—structure became ornament and architecture everywhere captured the worrisome whisper of the milieu like a pair of Depression era pants mended and then mended again—everything had to give value and contribute to productivity. It was a unique time to become a registered architect.

DDT

Photo credit: audubon.org

The inventor of DDT was awarded a Nobel Prize. Available for civilian use in 1945, DDT was the most powerful pesticide the world had ever known. It was powerful because it was indiscriminate, capable of killing hundreds of different kinds of insects at once. Developed in 1939, DDT was lauded for clearing the South Pacific islands of malaria-causing insects threatening the survival of U.S. troops in World War II.

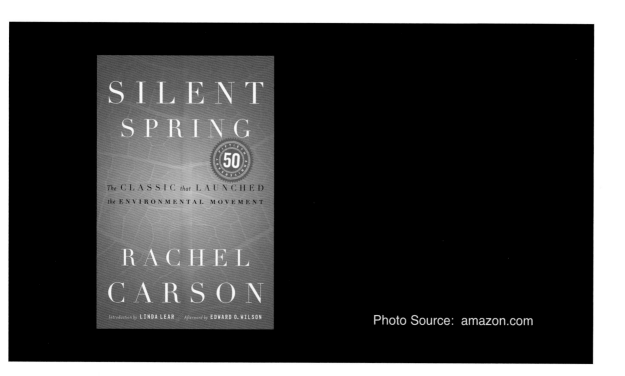

Photo Source: amazon.com

Biologist Rachel Carson's *Silent Spring* was one of the land-mark books of the 20th century tackling the issues of DDT. Her research proved that, rather than saving humanity from disease and pests, DDT entered the food chain via a network of pathways, causing enormous loss of animal life and affecting humans with cancer and other genetic damage. Presented as literature rather than a scientific report, her work caught the attention of the public and President John F. Kennedy, galvanizing the vulnerability of nature to human intervention and setting the stage for the environmental movement.

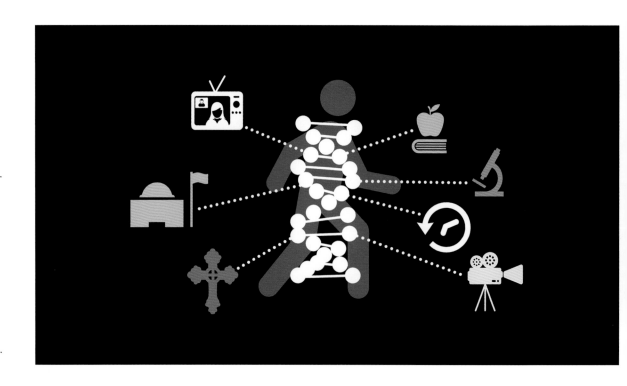

Systems theory posits that everything is interconnected and interdependent—the Big Circle of Life. Therefore, like the Butterfly Effect, changing just one thing, changes everything.

My parents were natural systems farmers before it was fashionable to be so. The farm was located across from a National Wildlife Refuge close to the Canadian border.

Dominated by a 360 degree line where land meets the sky, the late comedian Joan Rivers described the landscape as being "so flat you could see your relatives coming six months out."

Situated in the middle of the Bakken Formation with estimates
as high as 18 billion barrels of recoverable oil production, the
soil is rich and black both above and below that line.

Life as a farmer depended on the ability to read that sky, the wind, the wildlife and the landscape. When I arrived at Penn State I share boarded for the stables hosting the Penn State Equestrian team and one fall we had a very hard early frost. When I asked the stable owner if the horses had built up their hide, his reply was, "The smart ones did." 1500 acres is a large farm even in those parts, but they were never all in production at the same time. One-third would be planted with crops; another third would consist of fields of alfalfa restoring rich nitrogen to the soil to be bailed and sold for hay (perhaps to Montana ranchers); the other third would be summer fallowed to turn the alfalfa back into the earth eliminating the need to use chemical fertilizers.

We ate from our own gardens, livestock, and spring-fed well. Neighbors met together after church over strong coffee and organized labor and equipment sharing. Faith wasn't an option: a golden crop ready for harvest in a late summer morning could be destroyed that afternoon with a ten-minute hailstorm. Scandinavians aren't typically known for too much drama (or talking for that matter). Add to that parents who lived through the Depression and who survived WWII and were now raising a family in the '50s, nothing was wasted, and nothing was wrong. It's a license to be fearless.

design solved serious problems...

...learn about the world
find meaning
build a theology
manage resources

Photo Source: wikipedia.org

Therefore, Design solved serious problems; and Architecture had an aesthetic that originated in the realm of everyday life in which people create and negotiate their own sense of things— how they learn about the world, how they find meaning and build their own theology, how they manage the resources they love and depend upon.

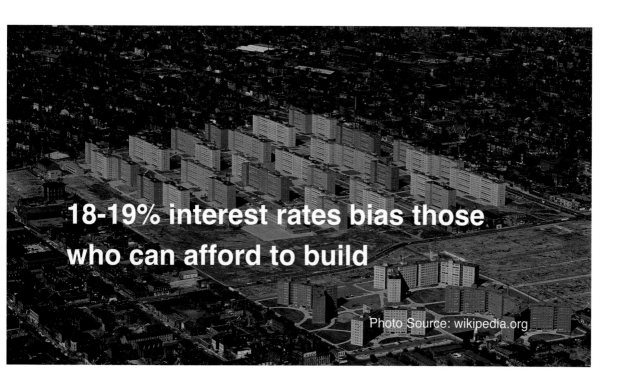

18-19% interest rates bias those who can afford to build

Photo Source: wikipedia.org

In my early days as an Architect, I saw interest rates as high 18 – 19%. That meant money was expensive and it biased only those who could afford to build—hospitals, universities, government. Absent was the sensibility and rootedness that emerges from Design detached from a Patron. And who was looking at how destructive and unsustainable Human Systems could be? We are the problem. I set out to be an Architect (big A) of architectures (little a) that recognized the social practices and the design of institutions that help us live as caring, connected, intelligent, and enlightened human beings.

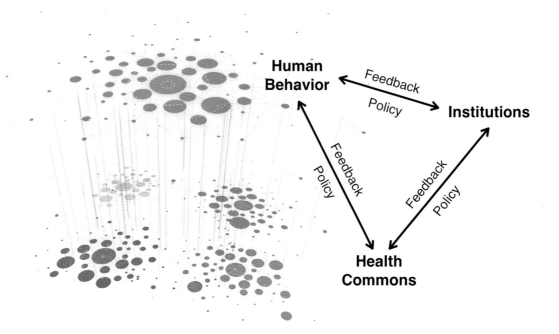

I developed a graduate seminar identifying Systems approaches to Commons environments, the institutions and human behavior associated with collective decision-making within community.

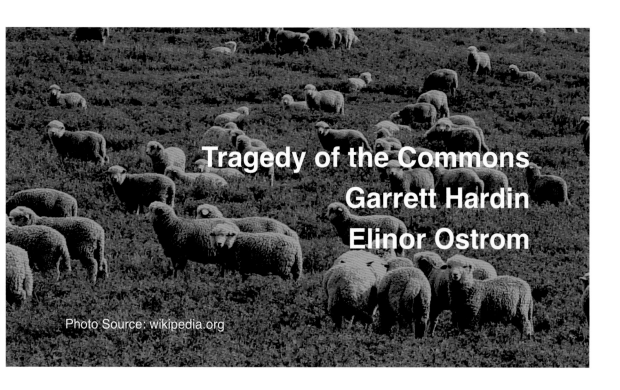

Tragedy of the Commons
Garrett Hardin
Elinor Ostrom

Photo Source: wikipedia.org

Darla V. Lindberg

Commons are typically associated with the "tragedy of the commons" parable. It holds that any shared resource invariably gets over-exploited as a result of self-interest. Since Hardin's famous essay in 1968, Commons topics have been identified in every discipline in an attempt to find better ways to effectively manage shared resources. A social scientist, Elinor Ostrom, won the Nobel Prize in Economics in 2009. Her work presented a case for grassroots approaches to institutional design impacting the Commons. Elinor passed away in 2012. Colleagues tell me Dr. Ostrom would be quite pleased with what an architect is doing to extend and expand her work.

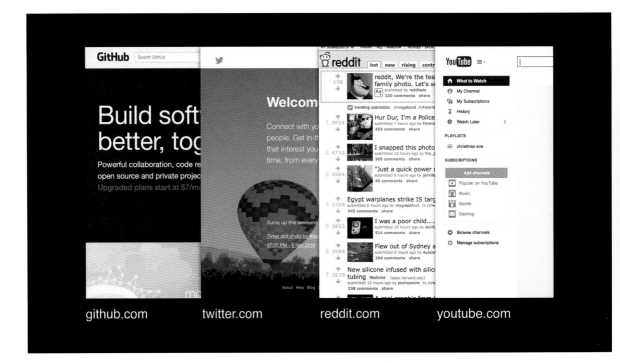

Commons like systems are packaged within community, with values, rules for operating and a worldview. And they are not limited to natural systems but can be seen in open source software (Git-Hub), social media (Twitter), and a range of shared virtual communities (Reddit)(YouTube).

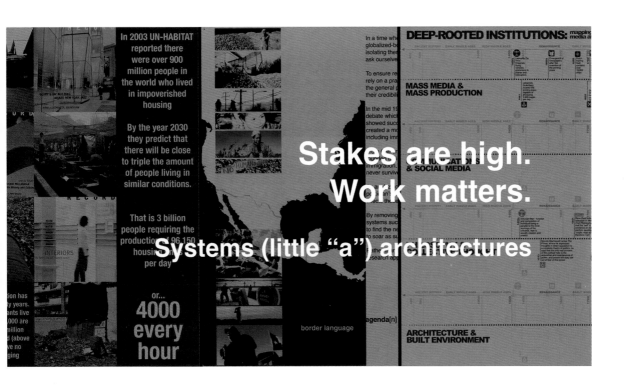

As a result of thinking of "architectures" (little "a") this way we have been invited to explore design solutions for problems exposing systems-wide failures. "Water seeks its own level" is a classic reference to Systems Thinking. "For most of us design is invisible. Until it fails." In fact, the secret ambition of design is to become invisible, to be taken up into the culture, absorbed into the background.

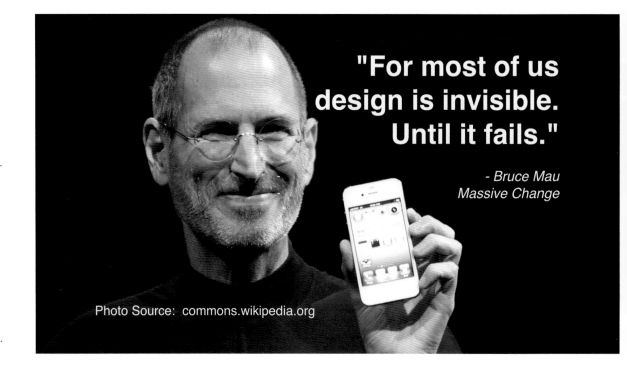

"For most of us design is invisible. Until it fails."

- Bruce Mau
Massive Change

Photo Source: commons.wikipedia.org

Apple, for example, is a company that has done more to make Design a part of our everyday lives than any Starchitect out there. They did that by targeting a technology like the telephone but then designed it for more than communication but included every aspect of our lives involving interaction. Systems Architecture innovates the familiar and changes everything in the process.

Worried Well.
Shock Value.

Photo Source: huffingtonpost.com,
wikipedia.org, globalnews.ca

We were asked to address recovery efforts after a natural, or unnatural disaster. First Responders are the emergency medical, police and fire—those first on the scene in an emergency. Compounding efforts of first responders are the "worried-well"—roughly 3500 out of every 5000 (or 70%)—who otherwise jam up medical, transportation and communication systems as emergency operations attempt to move into action. Still another kind of "pandemic" results from uncoordinated information.

Unfortunately the public has come to expect the media to profit from "shock value." Therefore, a means that might otherwise be ubiquitous, affordable and accessible goes underutilized by the public in these emergency situations.

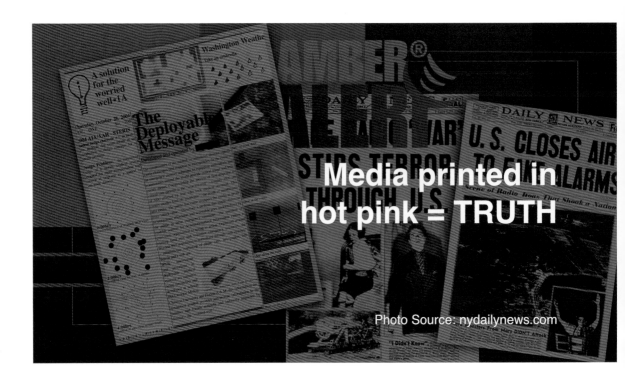

Media printed in hot pink = TRUTH

Photo Source: nydailynews.com

We designed "The Deployable Message," a networked communications system designed to override credible sources (newspapers, news magazines, print media) for de-sensationalized information in times of disaster and relief. Like the Amber Alert or the Emergency Broadcast Systems, the media is announced uniquely. In our case the media takes on the color of "hot pink" and is free.

Haiti Earthquake
January 12, 2010 / 7.0 magnitude
1.5 million people living in camps

Source: wikipedia.org

After the earthquake that hit Haiti in January of 2010 and the failing of the emergency camps in Corail, Haiti, we expanded the role of a Systems Response Infrastructure with what we called, the "Virtual Town Center."

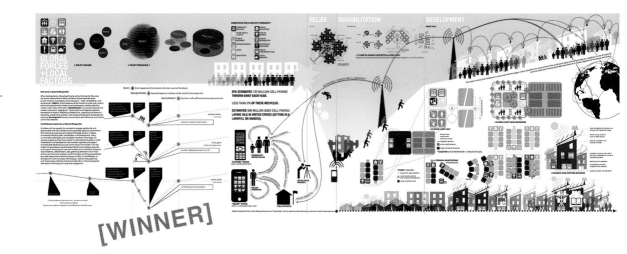

[WINNER]

Our innovation won us first prize in an "I Am a Second Respond-
er" competition. Our approach acknowledged that temporary
camps become permanent settlements. Lives are uprooted and
displaced. Starting over may also mean not going back.

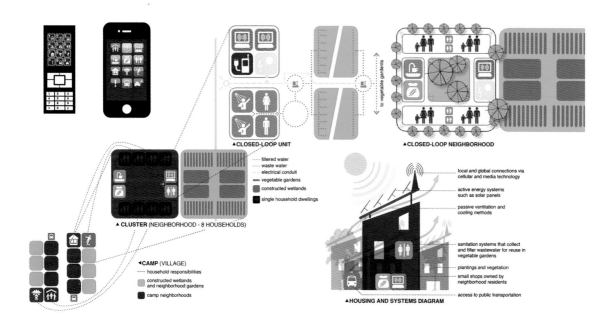

CLOSED-LOOP UNIT

CLOSED-LOOP NEIGHBORHOOD

to vegetable gardens

..... filtered water
..... waste water
..... electrical conduit
—— vegetable gardens
constructed wetlands
single household dwellings

CLUSTER (NEIGHBORHOOD - 8 HOUSEHOLDS)

CAMP (VILLAGE)
..... household responsibilities
constructed wetlands and neighborhood gardens
camp neighborhoods

local and global connections via cellular and media technology

active energy systems such as solar panels

passive ventilation and cooling methods

sanitation systems that collect and filter wastewater for reuse in vegetable gardens

plantings and vegetation

small shops owned by neighborhood residents

access to public transportation

HOUSING AND SYSTEMS DIAGRAM

We harnessed social media and cell-phone technology to call on second responders world-wide to assist in planning, design, construction, water, sanitation, energy, food, and transportation design needed to rebuild well.

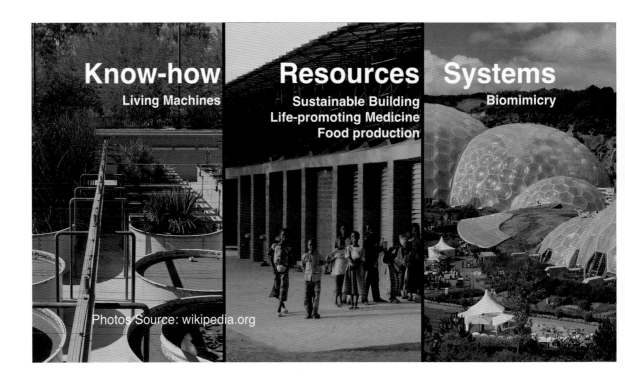

Know-how
Living Machines

Resources
Sustainable Building
Life-promoting Medicine
Food production

Systems
Biomimicry

Photos Source: wikipedia.org

The know-how is there; the resources are there;
the systems are simple.

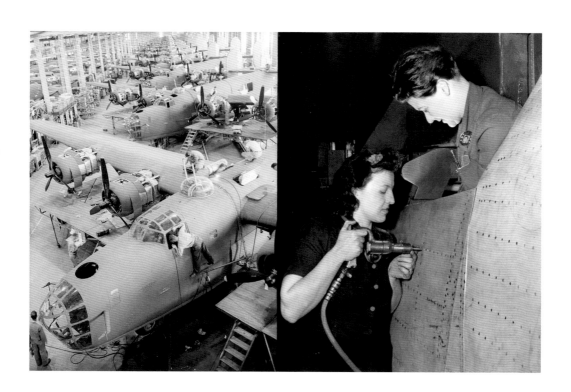

If Detroit could retool and retrain from automobiles to war in three years for WWII, and John Oliver and Reddit can combine to "fix" Net Neutrality rules in under 10 months, we can do this.

Japan Earthquake + Tsunami
March 11, 2011 / 9.0 magnitude

Photo Source: theglobeandmail.com

The idea of mobilizing global know-how through a virtual town center was reinforced after the earthquake and tsunami that collapsed the NE coastline of Honshu, Japan. With nuclear danger, friends and family on the inside asked a virtual community to rally and help orchestrate relief from positions around the world.

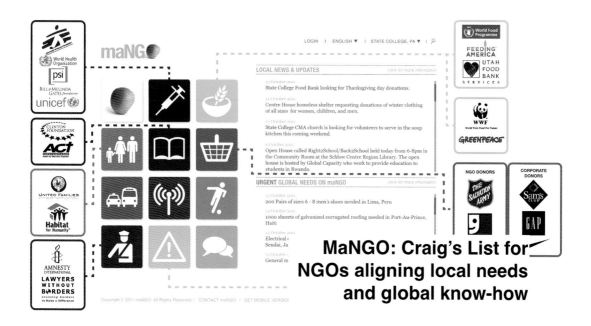

MaNGO: Craig's List for NGOs aligning local needs and global know-how

All these experiences have shaped a current web-based technology we refer to as MaNGO. The mango is an appropriate symbol. In many cultures around the world every part of the mango is used, consumed or revered. For us MaNGO is a "craigslist" for NGOs aligning local needs and global know-how.

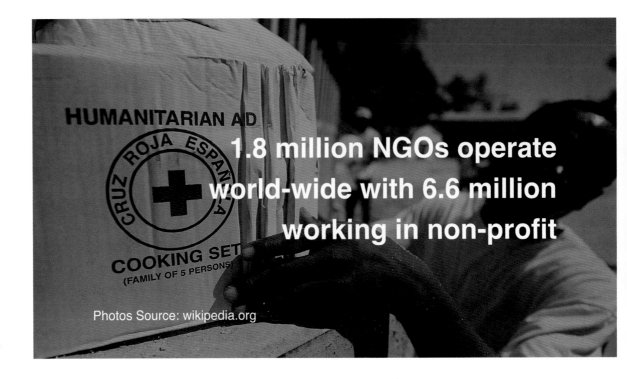

Photos Source: wikipedia.org

1.8 million NGOs operate worldwide but with 6.6 million individuals working in the non-profit sector,

Still inefficiency, mismanagement, lack of accountability and misappropriation of funds are unfortunate operational norms.

One of our team members lived and worked in Chilca, Peru. He saw clothing donations sent to a community in Peru only to find the clothes from North America were too large for the physically smaller Peruvians. They needed small shoes for small feet. And informal settlements around the world see NGOs arrive to build homes and infrastructure but leave with the work unfinished due to lack of real coordination with local expertise.

Concept illustration for MaNGO.

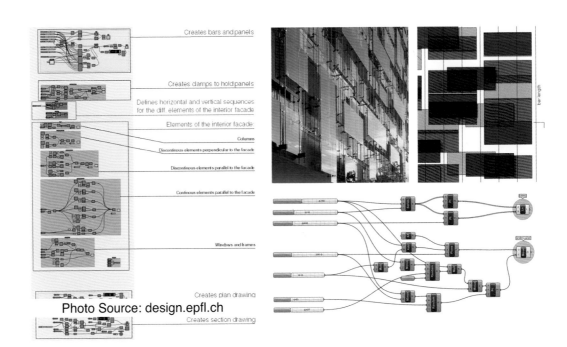

Creates bars and panels

Creates clamps to hold panels

Defines horizontal and vertical sequences for the diff. elements of the interior facade

Elements of the interior facade:

Columns

Discontinous elements perpendicular to the facade

Discontinous elements parallel to the facade

Continous elements parallel to the facade

Windows and frames

Creates plan drawing

Photo Source: design.epfl.ch

Creates section drawing

It leverages parametric building software—sophisticated modeling software used in Architecture for scenario building of parameters that optimize, for example, views, or core to glass, or materials and construction logistics for complex large-scale construction projects around the world.

MaNGO adapts that technology to grassroots efforts for self-building local practices in real time.

If our concept of social justice is founded on the framework of the public as a shared interest, then at-risk Commons are a reflection of the failing of that framework

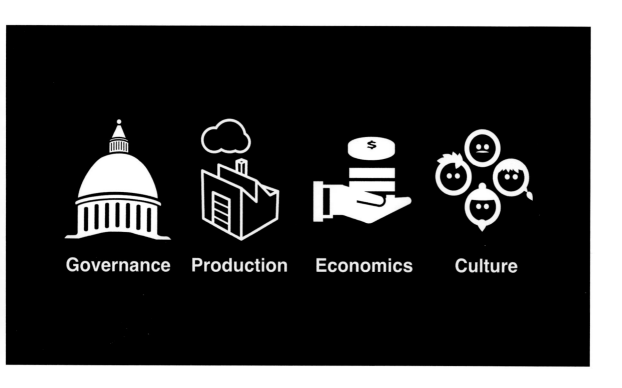

Governance **Production** **Economics** **Culture**

We need a reimagined integrated ecosystem of governance, production, economics and culture. While this may seem like a worldview that is out of sync with our current reductive processes of reason and logic, I say it is operating right now around us, only.

Darla V. Lindberg

**Participation
Inclusiveness
Fairness
Bottom-up control
Community-based innovation
Accountability**

Photos Source: wikipedia.org

The social practices of participation, inclusiveness, fairness, bottom-up control, community-based innovation, and account-ability. And, it's about honoring the role of life and metabolism and building a need for meaning and beauty and relevance in our models for policy reform. Recently, in my graduate seminar I found myself advising my students to dust off the kinds of questions we get from five year old children. Questions like, "so why can't cars fly?"

Photo Source: fanspot.com

thefancarpet

My favorite question of this sort is in the movie, *Matilda*, where Danny DeVito's character, Mr. Wormwood, Matilda's father, takes Matilda and her brother to his car dealership to show them the tricks to selling cars. Matilda is horrified to see her dad is passing off bad cars to innocent customers. She asks, "don't people need good cars, dad?" "Can't we sell good cars?"

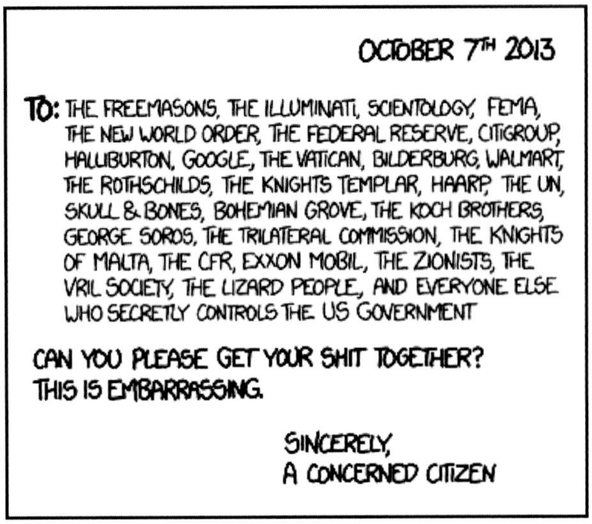

OCTOBER 7TH 2013

TO: THE FREEMASONS, THE ILLUMINATI, SCIENTOLOGY, FEMA, THE NEW WORLD ORDER, THE FEDERAL RESERVE, CITIGROUP, HALLIBURTON, GOOGLE, THE VATICAN, BILDERBURG, WALMART, THE ROTHSCHILDS, THE KNIGHTS TEMPLAR, HAARP, THE UN, SKULL & BONES, BOHEMIAN GROVE, THE KOCH BROTHERS, GEORGE SOROS, THE TRILATERAL COMMISSION, THE KNIGHTS OF MALTA, THE CFR, EXXON MOBIL, THE ZIONISTS, THE VRIL SOCIETY, THE LIZARD PEOPLE, AND EVERYONE ELSE WHO SECRETLY CONTROLS THE US GOVERNMENT

CAN YOU PLEASE GET YOUR SHIT TOGETHER? THIS IS EMBARRASSING.

SINCERELY, A CONCERNED CITIZEN

Photo Source: xkcd.com

And perhaps an adult version of Matilda's challenge might look like this.

Commons problems
Communal resources
Participatory governance
Generosity
Systems Thinking

Darla V. Lindberg

In closing, when my oldest son was in grade school I was invited to speak to his class during their Medieval Architecture module. I brought these two toys to illustrate the difference between Medieval Big "M" as a style involving castles, knights and jousting and medieval little "m" to denote the one-of-a-kind process of craft and making. It was very well received. The following week I received a bundle of delightful thank you notes from the students. One little girl summed up my TED talk...

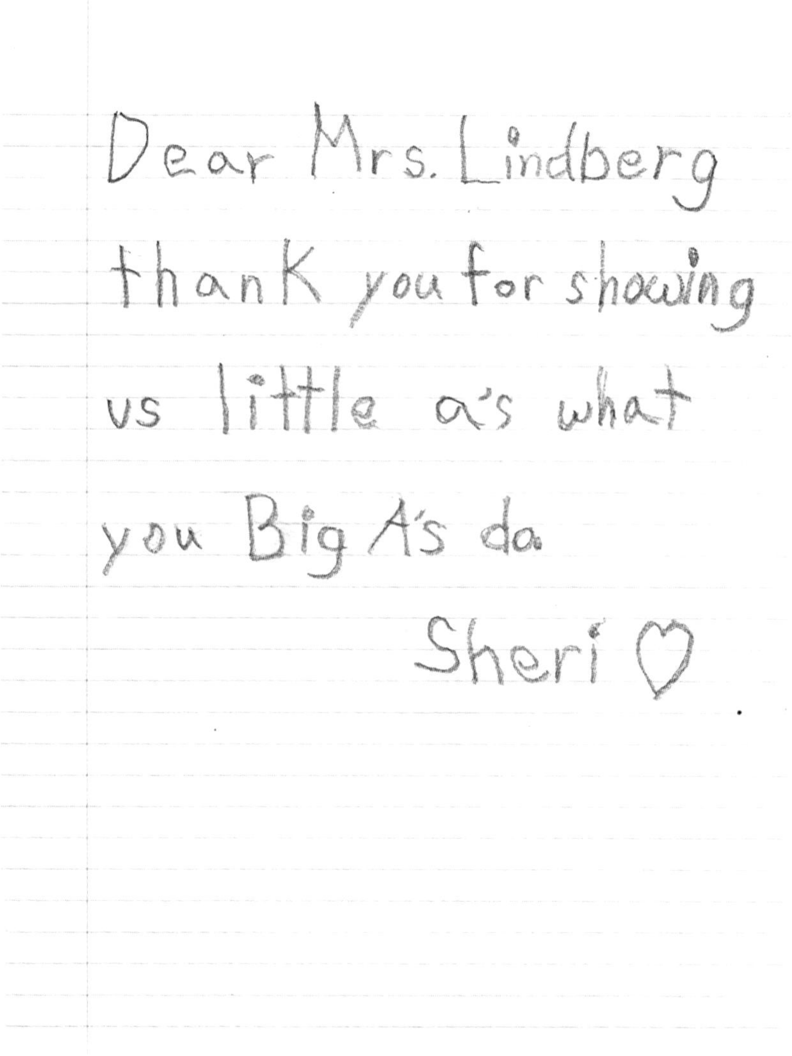

Dear Mrs. Lindberg
thank you for showing
us little a's what
you Big A's da
                Sheri ♡

In 2004, I was invited to an "invitation only" International Conference on Advances in the Internet (IPSI) in Pescara, Italy.[127] I took the opportunity to work through my thoughts on the fringe-to-the-center in my paper and presentation, "Emergent Architectures of Open Source: A Conjecture." The center-to-the-fringe commonly references a circle where the perimeter, the fringe, is rotating faster and faster depending on its distance from the center. This principle has been deployed on the bicycle wheel, in sports, in machines and nature. The larger the circle, the lesser the effort at the center to make the fringe create enormous momentum. Children playing "whip the tail" or participating in a Chinese Dragon know that the kids on the end of the tail will likely not be able to keep up as the tail grows longer and whips aggressively around curves and bends as they run through the street. The fringe-to-the-center also references any social, political, economic or art movement taking place remotely from the status quo. The recent interest by asset management firms and insurance companies and other heavily layered economies in blockchain technology is due to the rapid growth in value experienced by the fringe currency, BitCoin. For my presentation, I composed a simple tune on the piano, recorded it on a keyboard using GarageBand software and then proposed extending this to the world through the Internet for amateur musicians to offer up recorded demonstrations of how they might augment the piece. I imagined an eventual recording produced by David Bryne of the former post-punk band, Talking Heads or by the late Prince. This has been done by many amateur artists since then, but at the time it was a novel idea.

The physics of working out on the fringe where things are accelerated and harder to control also represents the rate of success of markets scaling up on Main Street. A small mom-and-pop shop relying on local pedestrian traffic stocks just enough merchandise to keep up with supply and demand for that local market. I once heard a story of a small shop in a small town in the upper Northeastern U.S. selling pine nuts on Main Street. Because a major highway went through their town, the pine nut shop scaled their business to selling to locals and to the tourists passing through. Once a bypass was built outside of town directing tourist traffic away from Main Street, the pine nut business suffered. Selling only to the local market wasn't enough to keep the shop making a profit. So, the pine nut shop built a website, opened their doors to the world through the Internet and the shop's business multiplied and flourished.

Economic and finance arbitrage result from the practice of taking advantage of a price difference between two or more markets. In principle, an arbitrage is risk-free since the price difference is driven by market demand and exposure. Obviously, advertising, presentation, quality and purpose all drive this demand in a local setting—your product may simply be better than your competition's. But getting the product(s) in front of a larger market is the easiest way to stimulate an arbitrage opportunity, even for a product of lesser quality. Relying on volume has become the standard way an entrepreneur makes a major profit as start-ups or privately run enterprises become publicly traded companies or sell to larger companies eager to eliminate the competition. The story of PayPal's founding and resistance to a hostile takeover is a classic example of this.[128] The more recent abuse of arbitrage opportunities is witnessed as lobbyists and special interest groups fund political figures willing to champion a cause. In 2010, the U.S. Supreme Court ruled in Citizens United v. Federal Election Commission, that laws preventing corporations and unions from using their general treasury funds for independent "electioneering communications" (political advertising) violated the First Amendment's guarantee of freedom of speech.[129] Immediately perceived as historically important, the decision generated intense controversy outside the court as an overreaching attempt to rewrite campaign finance law. Critics cried this decision would, "open the floodgates for special interests...to spend without limit in our elections." Arbitrage opportunities, like the end of the Chinese Dragon, are designed to move swiftly to drive momentum. Because arbitrage moves are on the fringe, they are not as well vetted, researched and tested. Instead, pure volume dominates the ability to advertise, persuade, promote and legislate a product or an idea. Thinking back on the Stag Hunt, depending on which side of the movement you are on, an arbitrage opportunity can make you a benefactor of the Stag Hunt, or a Fool left behind. The problem this creates for a world that approaches 10 billion people, prices for everything escalate making it impossible to not push for an arbitrage opportunity to make ends meet. When we apply this practice to every already overused and overextended Commons ecosystem and economy on the planet, the incidence of collapse in every market is inevitable.

Douglas Rushkoff, Professor of Media Theory and Digital Economics at CUNY/Queens has lectured and written about programs and programmers in a similar way. He argues that before there was money, there was social currency.[130] He describes how a local harvest had value for a particular community. They grew what their local climate and conditions would support and then developed a lifestyle around the range of products extracted from their place on earth. Every harvest was utilized from the kernel to the straw, the stubble and the root. Social currency facilitated the trade and exchange of items produced and services needed within the community. I could relate. Scandinavian churches, for instance, took on the craftsmanship of boat building reflecting the plentiful wood from the forest and the boatbuilding skills of the people. And entire communities coordinated labor for an upcoming harvest during an after-church conversation over coffee. But these self-reliant communities out on the fringe were difficult for any central government to control. So the Monarchy presented reasons why a central government was important to the independent fringe communities, i.e., an army to protect them from external threats, or a shipping industry to extend their products to a world-wide market. To coordinate this new shared economy, the Monarchy created a common coin and placed the ruler's face on it—the "coin of the realm" necessitating a central bank and uniform money currency for exchange. Efficiency at the small scale of Main Street, or fringe communities make only enough money to cover the costs of the enterprise and the people involved. Any musician selling millions of single records and making a few cents on each, or collecting royalties for every time a song is used, knows how compounding makes money. Compounding interest on investments or adding multiple franchises, or increasing the volume of sales are all ways to make massive amounts of money with small amounts of profit per sale. So, we see the pattern and we recognize the Stag Hunt once again. Big is better. Especially as far as following the money goes. Anything bigger requires more material, more people, more coordination. Big, then, is as much a function of how the money works as anything related to population increase. So, the trucks get bigger, cars get bigger, roads get bigger, cities get bigger, crop yields get bigger, meals get bigger, people get bigger *and sicker*, health care gets bigger, people live longer, and the world spins around.

When you follow the money, success never means planning for less. I'm reminded of the documentary *Who Killed the Electric Car?*[131] The film presents the history of the electric car as nothing new. But once the car companies realized there was no money in a maintenance free car, they helped to orchestrate its elimination. Students since have taken on the societal structural issue of working to become less dependent on oil as an architectural thesis. They soon also realize that as long as trillions of dollars are to be made by Stag Hunters extracting the coal, oil and gas remaining in the earth, the dream of a living cooperatively with renewable resources is to be the Fool.

Still more disconcerting, consider examples where a person or a non-profit creates a social setting with a willingness to take up the slack where other institutions are not doing their part. In the documentary *Walmart: the high cost of low price*,[132] it is revealed that employees are not given health care benefits and are threatened to lose their jobs if they work overtime and are encouraged to "use their taxpayer dollars" to utilize welfare and Medicaid.

Examples are everywhere. Universities raise tuition knowing most students and families will find a way to meet the increase. So students who are especially financially compromised take advantage of free meals at church dinners to offset this hardship. Churches, then, grow a community and further rely on that community to help others where other institutions, city and governmental services come up lean.

Following the money reveals still another psychological game. Hard times have always produced some of the biggest arbitrage opportunities in history. The 18th Amendment to the U.S. Constitution—known as the Prohibition Amendment—was adopted in the 1920s when times were good making the production, selling, possessing, and consuming of alcoholic drinks illegal.[133] Then in the early 1930s when alcohol was illegal, people would make their own. "Near" beer and other bootlegged products brought an increase in organized crime, especially in major cities. Gangs became more violent and the battle over turf and control of liquor sales and illegal activities that came along with it—prostitution and gambling—grew.

Economic downturn throughout the 1930s, WWI and WWII and the 1970s resulted in fashion trends reflecting frugality and a shift toward more masculine lines with longer hemlines, androgynous pants and less variety. Conversely, when economies improved as in the 1920s, '50s, '60s, '80s and '90s and the new millennium, prosperity generally brought shorter skirts, more diversity and expressive styles. Christian Dior, for example, launched his career in the late forties with a postwar pivot to bring back the feminine waist, a billowing skirt, excessive fabric, full layered tulle, exposing ankles and high heels, complemented by wide-brimmed hats and elaborate textures to dust off the malaise of hard times. The physics of the Big Bang teaches us nothing is too big to fail. Every day some institution becomes ripe for disruption and another giant falls.

Policy**Space:**
Groupthink trappings

PolicySpace may not be a familiar term in architecture and landscape architecture. Our domains are more comfortable with "urban theory" "urbanism" "politics of space" "social justice." We remain in our safe domain topics; we objectify the product and maintain tidy boundaries where disciplines own critical analysis of how things work. Complexity theory would encourage and actually demand enormous specificity. But it's the in the cracks between domains—between these disciplinary turfs (groupthink zones) where overlap is not theorized where the problems (historically and always) of abuse and exploitation occur.

PolicySpace:
Asymmetrical information

Asymmetrical information: the originator of the Lemon Law won a Nobel Prize, illustrating when one side knows more than the other, i.e., the car dealer, the sales man.

Pearl Harbor: the reaction when you make someone a social sucker (game theory).

Bay of Pigs: trusting administrative leadership (Cuban Missile Crisis started in Eisenhower administration and blindly carried out in Kennedy administration).

Milgram Experiment: no one questioned the office or the decisions of another authority.

Watergate Cover Up: one side deciding just what the truth ought to be.

Orson Welles, "War of the Worlds": information on the radio was supposed to be truth.

PolicySpace:
Social media, Wall Street, the "hive mind"

Groupthink: especially exploited with the advancement of Social media.
Wall Street: we trust others with oversight of the way things work.
The "Hive Mind": setting cultural memes. A collection of "trending now" themes.

PolicySpace:
Leveraging design and meaningful community participation

Darla V. Lindberg

Breaking out of groupthink takes risks. In Game Theory, the best test of a strategy is to play a move on itself. If it worked to do harm, it can also work to do good.

Policy**Space:**
Using social media to create awareness

Manibeli Declaration

Date: Thursday, September 1, 1994

Calling for a Moratorium on World Bank Funding of Large Dams

WHEREAS:

1. The World Bank is the greatest single source of funds for large dam construction, having provided more than U.S.$50 billion (1992 dollars) for construction of more than 500 large dams in 92 countries. Despite this enormous investment, no independent analysis or evidence exists to demonstrate that the financial, social and environmental costs were justified by the benefits realized;

2. Since 1948, the World Bank has financed large dam projects which have forcibly displaced on the order of ten million people from their homes and lands. The Bank's own 1994 "Resettlement and Development" review admits that the vast majority of women, men and children evicted by Bank–funded projects never regained their former incomes nor received any direct benefits from the dams for which they were forced to sacrifice their homes and lands. The Bank has consistently failed to implement and enforce its own policy on forced resettlement, first established in 1980, and despite several policy reviews the Bank has no plans to fundamentally change its approach to forced resettlement;

3. The World Bank is planning to fund over the next three years 18 large dam projects which will forcibly displace another 450,000 people, without any credible guarantee that its policy on resettlement will be enforced. Meanwhile the Bank has no plans to properly compensate and rehabilitate the millions displaced by past Bank–funded dam projects, including populations displaced since 1980 in violation of the Bank's policy;

4. World Bank–funded large dams have had extensive negative environmental impacts, destroying forests, wetlands, fisheries, and habitat for threatened and endangered species,

Related Information

Programs and Campaigns (2)

  › Banks and Dam Builders
  › World Bank Group

Contact Us

› Zachary Hurwitz
  zachary@internationalrivers.org
  +1 (510) 848-1155 ext. 313

Manibeli Declaration: We can use social media to create awareness as in the Game Theory narrative, Belling the Cat.

PolicySpace:

Humor – powerful and disarming - for a wide audience

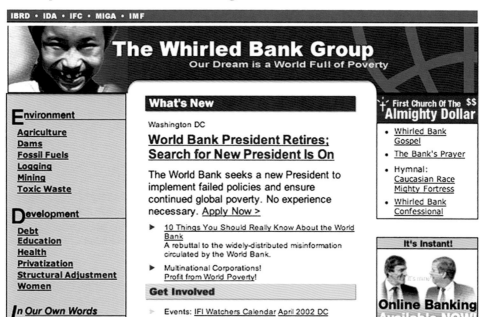

Humor: powerful and disarming for a wide audience.

Policy**Space:**
Marshaling an arsenal of expertise from every domain

REBUILD BY DESIGN

An Initiative of the President's Hurricane Sandy Rebuilding Task Force	Lead Supporter The Rockefeller Foundation
In Collaboration With NYU's Institute for Public Knowledge Municipal Art Society Regional Plan Association Van Alen Institute	With Support From Deutsche Bank Americas Foundation Hearst Foundation Surdna Foundation The JPB Foundation The New Jersey Recovery Fund

Rebuild by Design: Innovating Together to Create a Resilient Region

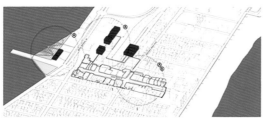

After three months of research and conversation with communities in New York, New Jersey, Connecticut, and beyond, the Department of Housing and Urban Development (HUD) has selected 10 projects across the Sandy-affected region to be pursued in the next and final stage of the Rebuild by Design competition. Share your views on these thoughtful, unique visions for a more resilient region, and check out streaming video of the October

MANAGE Tie financing to capacity-building for a newly-formed merchants' association.

FINANCE Create an innovative resiliency fund seeded with federal funds and incorporating capital from financial institutions to support business improvements.

It involves the marshaling of an arsenal of expertise from every domain. And because this is not easy, requiring a new battery of tools and skills sets, we feel strongly this calls for a new kind of expert designer—one that works the seams of systems of law, environment, media, finance, resources and are owned by corporations controlling oil, water, information, global finance and conflict.

PolicySpace:
Uncompromising design fully aware of the rules and the fine print

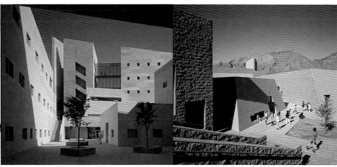

Uncompromising design fully aware of the rules and the fine print—innovating with data to address low budget, high risk, public housing, grade schools, and theatres.

Michael Pyatok: Ocean Avenue project in San Francisco
Coop Himmelblau: UFA Cinema Center in Dresden, Germany
Antoine Predock: Science Canyon

Protecting the health, safety and welfare of our users is paramount to our professional code—it's fundamental before anything else. Ought we not also know how to do this when it comes to interpreting the regulatory mechanisms that shape our cities, outline expansion and development, including land use?

Policy**Space**

Based on generalization of advancement of industry in the western world throughout the 20th century, Lefebvre was concerned with the deep transformation of the city into a complete urbanization of society.

Works such as those of **Henri Lefebvre** have deeply influenced the development of urban theory and urban formation around the world. Based on a generalization of the advancement of industry in the western world throughout the twentieth century, his writings were concerned with the deep transformation of the city into a complete urbanization of society. Widely recognized as a Marxist thinker, themes as "the right to the city" and "the urban revolution" in Lefebvre's writings were especially influential to human geography, as witnessed by both his Neo-Marxist supporters and his Postmodern critics.

Policy**Space**

Influential authors such as **David Harvey, Dolores Hayden,**
and **Edward Soja** anticipated the city would reach a point
where it could no longer support the democratized space
and worried openly about the privatization of the public.
The L.A. Riots (Race Wars) of the early '90s (also caught on
video and played back in real time) reinforced policy efforts
to privatize the public.

Policy**Space**

Collective action is difficult. Institutional products as a result of collective action tend to remain the same or go unchallenged due to lack of organized or formal mechanisms to challenge. Both "hard" and "soft" systems of infrastructure development remain deeply grounded in this bias toward 20th century urbanization, yet global stressors are challenging this paradigm at multiple scales.

And given the difficulty in collective action, institutional products tend to remain resistant to change, both the "hard" (roads, utilities, communication) and "soft" (regulating, governing, financing, specializing systems), infrastructure development remain steeply grounded in this bias toward twentieth century urbanization.

Policy**Space**

110TH CONGRESS
1ST SESSION **S. 1926**

To establish the National Infrastructure Bank to provide funding for qualified
infrastructure projects, and for other purposes.

IN THE SENATE OF THE UNITED STATES
AUGUST 1, 2007

Mr. DODD (for himself and Mr. HAGEL) introduced the following bill, which
was read twice and referred to the Committee on Banking, Housing, and
Urban Affairs

A BILL

To establish the National Infrastructure Bank to provide
funding for qualified infrastructure projects, and for
other purposes.

1   *Be it enacted by the Senate and House of Representa-*
2   *tives of the United States of America in Congress assembled,*
3   **SECTION 1. SHORT TITLE; TABLE OF CONTENTS.**
4   (a) SHORT TITLE.—This Act may be cited as the
5   "National Infrastructure Bank Act of 2007".
6   (b) TABLE OF CONTENTS.—The table of contents of
7   this Act is as follows:

    Sec. 1. Short title; table of contents.
    Sec. 2. Findings.
    Sec. 3. Definitions.
    Sec. 4. Authorization of appropriations.

Clean and Green Tax Break: Developers build starter-castles to pay roll-back taxes for seven years since land use changes

The general rule of the Clean and Green program is that after land is enrolled, the landowner is obligated to continue using the land in a qualified use indefinitely or face the penalty of roll-back taxes for the most recent seven years, plus interest. The roll-back tax is the difference between the taxes paid based on the Clean and Green rate and the taxes that would have been paid if the land were not enrolled in Clean and Green. Roll-back taxes are due for the year of the change of use and the six previous tax years for a total of seven years. Land that has been in Clean and Green for more than seven years is only subject to roll-back taxes for the seven most recent tax years, and, land that has been in Clean and Green for less than seven years is subject to roll-back taxes only for the years it has been in the program. In addition to the tax, interest is imposed on each year's roll-back tax at the rate of six percent per year.

Tax Increment Financing (TIF): Financing Infrastructure for Fraser Center and other owner-occupied house, State College, PA

[4] Tax increment financing districts (TIFs) are used in Chicago as well as in many other cities and states. Typically, a specific geographic area is defined as "blighted" or in need of economic assistance. Once created, an annual tax revenue benchmark is established. Over the life of the TIF (typically 23 years), any tax revenue received over this benchmark is earmarked for use on TIF improvements. These can include community infrastructure enhancement, building improvements, residential or business construction, or other public benefits such as parks. Close to 30 percent of Chicago currently falls in a TIF (Neighborhood Capital Budget Group 2005) and at $329.5 million, TIF district revenues represent one-third of the City's total property tax income (Hinz 2005). More information is available at Neighborhood Capital Budget Group (2005) and City of Chicago (2005).

Characteristic of this, a landmark bill, The National Infrastructure Bank Act of 2007 would provide for a national fund to help pay for large infrastructure projects in the United States. On the surface this seems like a critical savings account to fund our deteriorating urban infrastructure, right? It's a solution that would make sense to any family or individual planning to finance replacement parts. But a closer look at the processes reveals this locks in the design of "hard" regularized systems to support the current paradigm of urban development and institutionalizes the "soft" processes to secure access to them (taxes, suggesting ownership). And the mechanisms for designing and reimagining the city, i.e., closed loop systems are out of reach.

Clean and Green Tax Law (PA); Environmental or Agricultural Easements elsewhere. Australia takes a very different approach given the finite amount of land. Consider the effects of social cleansing affected by ***Tax Increment Financing (TIF)***. Consider the relationship of unauthorized immigrants with jobs in the United States funding Social Security

Policy**Space**
A zeitgeist of sustainable development blurring/erase all boundaries

So, if the late 20th century zeitgeist—a spirit of the age that pervades culture, academic thought and politics—suggests sustainable development involving efforts to cross physical, social, cultural, economic, and political boundaries is essential, then a new kind of social analysis that looks beyond the confines of modern social theory to offer a more emancipatory alternative is required.

Policy**Space**
Calling for a more emancipated social theory

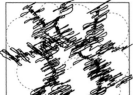

1 PolicySpace dynamics: systems feedbacks inform critical design

2 Designing with feedbacks: connecting top down + grassroots

3 Coining vulnerable "Data Commons" for design relevance

If "data" is the information we depend on flowing between systems … how we view it, how we understand it, and how we participate in it is critical for our survival as a just social system.

Darla V. Lindberg

PolicySpace
Policy Designs that Favor:
STABILITY

Policy Space
Policy Designs that Favor:
DYNAMICS

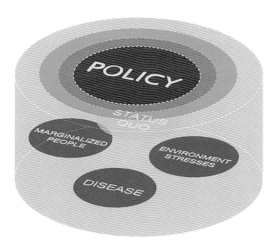

POLICY

STATUS QUO

MARGINALIZED PEOPLE

ENVIRONMENT STRESSES

DISEASE

equal voice
for America's families

voces unidas
para nuestras familias

I AM A SECOND RESPONDER [Winner]
Relief, Rehabilitation, and Development

RELIEF ① First response at the moment of crisis, survival handouts

REHABILITATION ② Second response initiates rehab, tools for development

DEVELOPMENT ③ Resilient, self-sufficient community networks

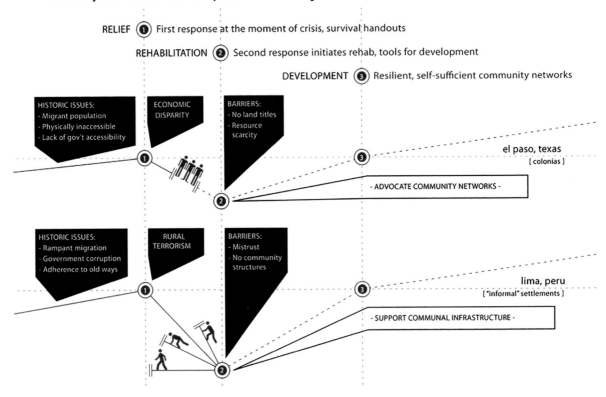

HISTORIC ISSUES:
- Migrant population
- Physically inaccessible
- Lack of gov't accessibility

ECONOMIC DISPARITY

BARRIERS:
- No land titles
- Resource scarcity

el paso, texas
[colonias]

- ADVOCATE COMMUNITY NETWORKS -

HISTORIC ISSUES:
- Rampant migration
- Government corruption
- Adherence to old ways

RURAL TERRORISM

BARRIERS:
- Mistrust
- No community structures

lima, peru
["informal" settlements]

- SUPPORT COMMUNAL INFRASTRUCTURE -

I AM A SECOND RESPONDER [Winner]
Virtual "Town Center"

EPA ESTIMATES 130 MILLION CELL PHONES THROWN AWAY EACH YEAR.

LESS THAN 2% OF THESE RECYCLED.

ESTIMATED 500 MILLION USED CELL PHONES LAYING IDLE IN UNITED STATES (SITTING IN A LANDFILL OR UNUSED).

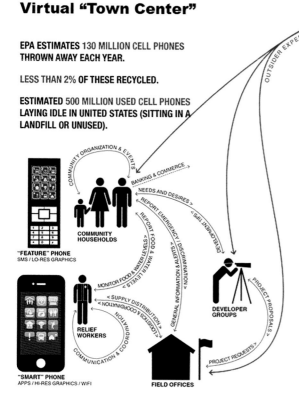

Using an innovative deployable and recyclable cell-phone technology, we proposed a virtual "town center" to connect communities in relief/ rehabilitation/ and development with outsider expertise and support. A coordinated infrastructure such as the virtual "town center" can help bridge the gap between local emergent dynamics and global expertise and support.

I AM A SECOND RESPONDER [Winner]
Closed-Loop Camps to Closed-Loop Neighborhoods

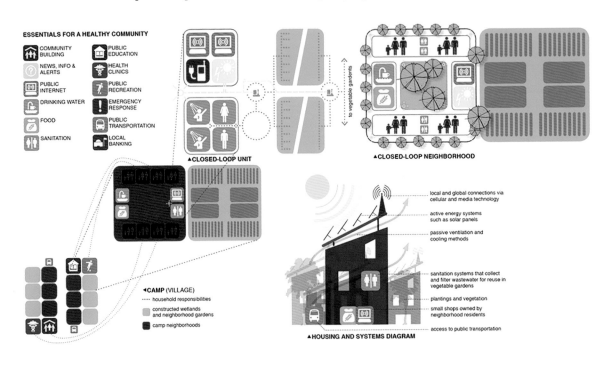

ESSENTIALS FOR A HEALTHY COMMUNITY

- COMMUNITY BUILDING
- NEWS, INFO & ALERTS
- PUBLIC INTERNET
- DRINKING WATER
- FOOD
- SANITATION
- PUBLIC EDUCATION
- HEALTH CLINICS
- PUBLIC RECREATION
- EMERGENCY RESPONSE
- PUBLIC TRANSPORTATION
- LOCAL BANKING

▲CLOSED-LOOP UNIT

▲CLOSED-LOOP NEIGHBORHOOD

◄CAMP (VILLAGE)
- ---- household responsibilities
- constructed wetlands and neighborhood gardens
- camp neighborhoods

local and global connections via cellular and media technology

active energy systems such as solar panels

passive ventilation and cooling methods

sanitation systems that collect and filter wastewater for reuse in vegetable gardens

plantings and vegetation

small shops owned by neighborhood residents

access to public transportation

▲HOUSING AND SYSTEMS DIAGRAM

HAITI IDEAS COMPETITION
"Model" Camps and Policy Failure

Lessons learned after the January 12, 2010 earthquake that struck Haiti reveal poorly coordinated recovery efforts, compounded by a lack of political will, the onset of hurricane season, and a cholera outbreak significantly challenged even the best NGO efforts at providing relief camps. Camp Corail-Cesselesse, Haiti was one such "model" camp. Designed to provide a new home for approximately 5000 people, the camp's reliance on approaches to urban infrastructure with a bias toward twentieth century determinate planned growth attracted an indeterminate pattern of squatter behavior outside its borders.

HAITI IDEAS COMPETITION
Closed-Loop Unit

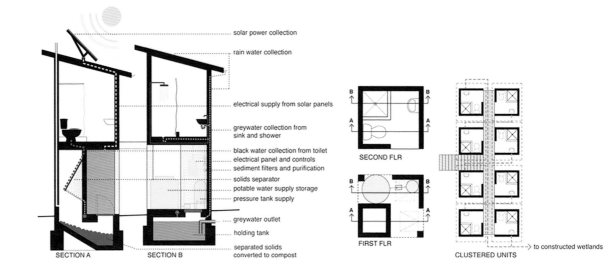

solar power collection

rain water collection

electrical supply from solar panels

greywater collection from
sink and shower

black water collection from toilet
electrical panel and controls
sediment filters and purification
solids separator
potable water supply storage
pressure tank supply

greywater outlet

holding tank

separated solids
converted to compost

SECTION A   SECTION B

SECOND FLR

FIRST FLR

CLUSTERED UNITS

B   B

A   A

B   B

A   A

to constructed wetlands

HAITI IDEAS COMPETITION
New Corail Camp Plan Using Closed-Loop Planning Strategies

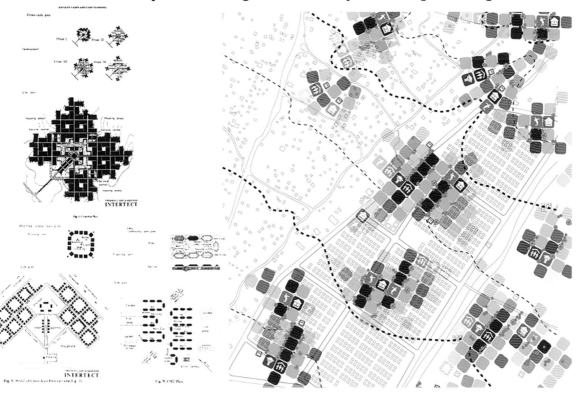

MaNGO

The NGO Problem

Our motivation: address frustrations and failures on both sides of aid distribution through readily available technologies.

Example: a U.S. nonprofit generously donates used clothing and shoes to an orphanage in Chilca, Peru, assuming they are aiding development. Yet the donations are much too large for the (physically smaller) women and children who desperately need them. Without credible feedback, the ill informed nonprofit in the U.S. continues to ship over-sized, unusable clothing to the orphanage.

MaNGO
The "Grasshopper" Approach

Grasshopper [GC] links families in need, suppliers, and community donation organizations through filtered information transferred directly to applicable responders. Data is transferred instantaneously from families in need to a corresponding supplier. By replacing current systems of miscommunication and delay, urgent needs can be communicated and supplies transferred by re-writing the output languages to appropriate levels of business/economic cognition. All information is non-destructive and can be re-routed at anytime based on live input.

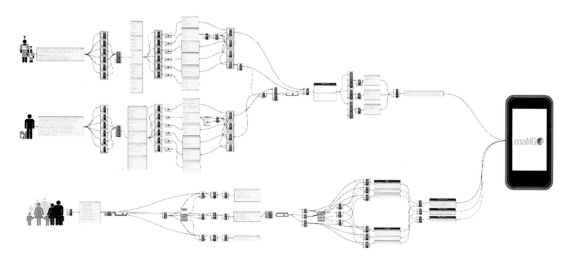

Darla V. Lindberg

MaNGO
The Ideal Outcome

Ma-NGO empowers anyone using a feature phone (SMS), smart phone or mobile technology to coordinate their own needs, servicing self-built income initiatives to build and restore local markets and livelihoods in times of rebuilding or development.

The result is a powerful smart and fast system able to absorb any data stored in a server, analyze it, and generate coordinated "matches" of outsider NGO resources, supplies, and skills directly to needs on the ground.

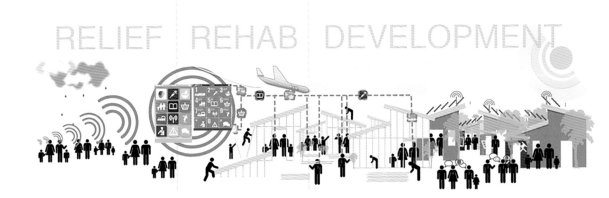

Gates Global Challenges
Grand Challenges in Global Health

"Grand Challenges in Global Health is a family of grant programs focused on one unifying purpose: To overcome persistent bottlenecks in creating new tools that can radically improve health in the developing world."

- GrandChallenges.org

11 Years : 45 Grants : $458 Million : Interdisciplinary Teams in 33 Countries
+
900 grants : $100,000 Each : Interdisciplinary Teams in 50 Countries

#10 LIMIT DRUG RESISTANCE
GRAND CHALLENGE **#1 IMPROVE VACCINES**
#5 SOLVE HOW TO DESIGN ANTIGENS
FOR EFFECTIVE, PROTECTIVE IMMUNITY
#15 DISCOVER BIOMARKERS #16 DISCOVER NEW WAYS
TO ACHIEVE HEALTHY BIRTH,
OF HEALTH AND DISEASE GROWTH, AND DEVELOPMENT
#11 CREATE THERAPIES THAT CAN CURE LATENT INFECTION
#9 CREATE A FULL RANGE OF **#12 CREATE** #3 DEVELOP NEEDLE-FREE DELIVERY SYSTEMS
OPTIMAL, BIOAVAILABLE NUTRIENTS
IN A SINGLE STAPLE PLANT SPECIES IMMUNOLOGICAL
METHODS THAT CAN CURE
CHRONIC INFECTIONS
#8 DEVELOP A CHEMICAL STRATEGY TO DEPLETE OR INCAPACITATE A DISEASE-TRANSMITTING INSECT POPULATION

Gates Immunization Dilemma
Create Low-Cost Cell Phone-Based Solutions for Improved Uptake and Coverage of Childhood Vaccinations

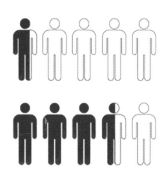

Vaccine-preventable diseases account for 14 percent of deaths in children under the age of 5 years. Millions more survive but live with severe impairments from disease.

the UN predicts that cell-phone ownership will reach [70% of the global population] in 2010.

Focuses of Challenge:

+ Positively identifying an individual infant/child for developing world vaccination programs.

+ Rapidly determining the immune status of an infant/child at the point of vaccination.

+ Connecting vaccine availability with target populations.

Gates Immunization Dilemma
Proposal: Iris Recognition Software for Medical Record Keeping

[infant arrives] [capture iris] [generate code] [256 byte iris code] [send to cloud] [certify match] [receive record] [give care]

Developing a universally recognizable language for cell-phone users, programmers, health care providers and patients using and advancing iris recognition biometrics technology for the purpose of promoting management of childhood vaccinations.

Gates Sanitation Dilemma
Challenge: Create the Next Generation of Sanitation Technologies

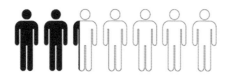 2.1 Billion People (33% of the global population) use non-sewered sanitation technologies that are unsustainable and detrimental to public health

Focuses of Challenge:

+ Hygienic and adequate pit/tank emptying and extraction

+ Recovery of energy from fecal sludge as a means for safe and affordable treatment and disposal

+ Appropriate sanitation solutions for areas challenged by an abundance of water (seasonal flooding, high groundwater tables, tidal communities, etc.)

+ Easy to clean, attractive and affordable latrine pan / squatting platform technologies that enhance latrines.

Gates Sanitation Dilemma
Proposal: A Decentralized, Closed-Loop Sanitation System

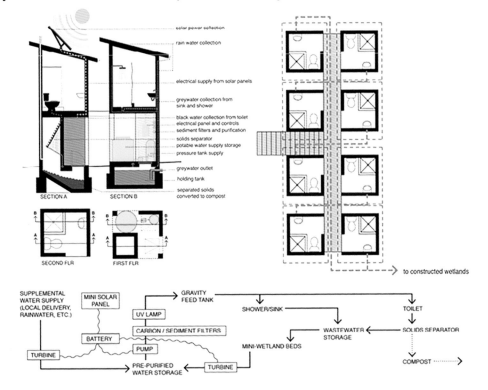

Gates Vaccination Dilemma
Challenge: Create more effective ways to assess local demands

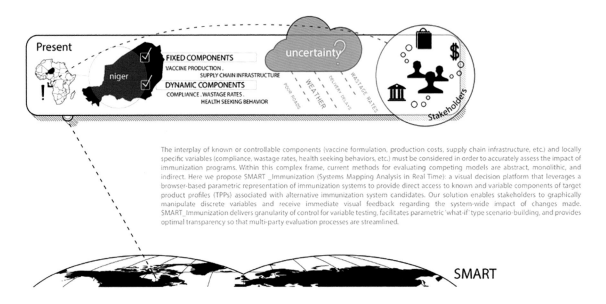

The interplay of known or controllable components (vaccine formulation, production costs, supply chain infrastructure, etc.) and locally specific variables (compliance, wastage rates, health seeking behaviors, etc.) must be considered in order to accurately assess the impact of immunization programs. Within this complex frame, current methods for evaluating competing models are abstract, monolithic, and indirect. Here we propose SMART _Immunization (Systems Mapping Analysis in Real Time): a visual decision platform that leverages a browser-based parametric representation of immunization systems to provide direct access to known and variable components of target product profiles (TPPs) associated with alternative immunization system candidates. Our solution enables stakeholders to graphically manipulate discrete variables and receive immediate visual feedback regarding the system-wide impact of changes made. SMART_Immunization delivers granularity of control for variable testing, facilitates parametric 'what-if' type scenario-building, and provides optimal transparency so that multi-party evaluation processes are streamlined.

SMART

Gates Vaccination Dilemma
Proposal: Create data driven directives based on domain expertise and localized disparate data involving site, weather, roads, variables

complexity does not arise from a complicated whole but rather a *lack of comparative similarity* between it's parts

Darla V. Lindberg

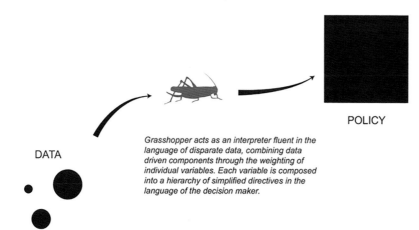

POLICY

DATA

Grasshopper acts as an interpreter fluent in the language of disparate data, combining data driven components through the weighting of individual variables. Each variable is composed into a hierarchy of simplified directives in the language of the decision maker.

Oxford Round Table
Critical Public Issues: Sentinel Cities

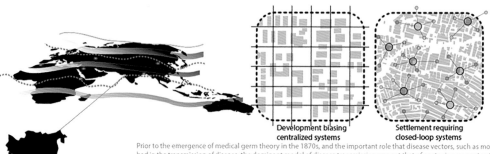

Khar West
Dhavari

Mumbai, India

Development biasing
centralized systems

Settlement requiring
closed-loop systems

Prior to the emergence of medical germ theory in the 1870s, and the important role that disease vectors, such as mosquitoes, lice, and birds had in the transmission of disease, the dominant model of disease transmission was not that of contagion, or contamination, but that people were believed to become sick from the noxious air produced by the places where they lived. It was not so much people, therefore, but places that were sick. The focus of medical attention was consequently away from anatomy to ecology, away from the study of the body as the locus of disease to the analysis of the disease-bearing aspects of physical environments. So, in addressing the question of global health, it needs to be understood that issues of expansion or national association were determined, or at least underwritten, by a tacit acceptance of a medical geography which submitted the most important question to ask of a country was not, "are they pleasant?" or "are they strategic?" but are they "healthy or not?" So, throughout the 1800s, questions of national wellbeing and global strength could not be separate from questions of health and morbidity. So for anyone in the nineteenth century, imagining disease was very much a part of imagining place. This paper presents an original thesis wherein globalization still operates with a tacit understanding of medical geography held over from the 1800s rendering borders a global xenophobic threat. Consequently, global disease management as a function of intact geopolitical bodies does not recognize mobility, epidemics and shared disasters. Investigating some of the fastest growing settlements in the world – also located by medical cartographers as among the deadliest miasmas – "Sentinel Cities" ponders the various systems representing a shifting paradigm in global disease management more characteristic of a world of porous borders.

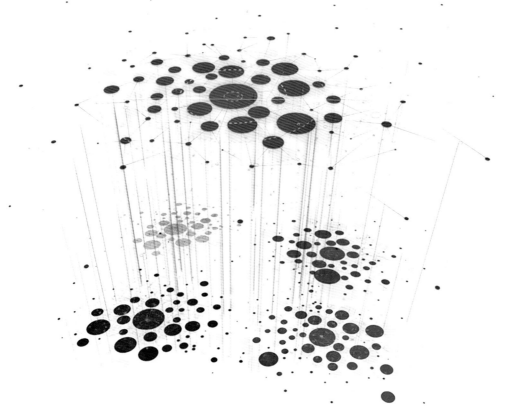

POLICYSPACE

PREPARING FOR THE HARVEST

PREPARING FOR THE HARVEST
The implement

This brings us to a look at a final Game 5.[134] In my graduate seminar, after we've read all the scholarly materials, walked through the logic and math of Game 1 (the initial Cheat), Game 2 (the perfect external agent with complete information), Game 3 (the imperfect external agent with incomplete information), and Game 4 (the Watcher of the Watcher), witnessed reality of the theories and models play out in excellently done documentaries, and discussed a wide range of examples by students from around the world, we are invigorated. We study the math closely, consider our options, and come to the realization we were actually better off with Game 1 than we are with Games 2 through 4. And now that we have strained relations with our neighbors, communication and coordination is virtually impossible and benefiting costly litigation. We've overlayed my Fairness Framework, witnessing through several scholarly articles and documentaries the dynamic relationship between Commons Environments, Institutions and Human Behavior associated with self-interest and cooperation. This is the policy arena for collective decision making affecting the entire system. So, we step back and consider this. The worst that happened in Game 1 was the initial Cheat. Original Sin was written into the story of our creation.[135] It's our human nature to mess up. The question becomes, what if we simply considered that initial Cheat as, good information? In the same way we work to "break" the code or "test" the experiment, can we rewrite the rules in order to make the framework more robust and resilient to inevitable flux and change?

The Case Studies selected here are examples of courageous student work. Deploying all the insights from the material covered in the semester, they pursued a topic of their own interest. Beautifully illustrated and thoroughly researched, their proposals exposed opportunities for institutional redesign making a case for grassroots, community-financed and locally managed institutions. The Case Studies reveal how tools for grappling with some of society's largest structural issues are a function of design, but with good information. And that information is only useful if it comes from a part-to-the-whole systems approach including expert knowledge from credible sources.

BIOGRAPHIES AND CASE STUDIES

David Maple received his Bachelor of Architecture from The Pennsylvania State University in 2007, and his Master of Science in Advanced Architectural Design (MSAAD) from Columbia University GSAPP in 2010. He is currently a Registered Architect in New York, is a Project Architect at Weiss/Manfredi Architects, and has been involved in international research and studies in Italy, Jordan and Brazil.

Sara Pettit received her Bachelor of Architecture from The Pennsylvania State University in 2009. She is a registered architect and lives and works in Philadelphia, PA. Her architectural thesis explored the urban fabric of Philadelphia, particularly the boundary conditions related to the processes of gentrification, population flight, urban decay and renewal. She has led design teams for a variety of institutional, commercial and governmental projects across the continental U.S. Outside of the studio, Sara's interests include mentoring high school students through the ACE mentoring program, renovating a 1859s rowhome with her Preservation Architect husband, and spending time with their young daughter, or engrossed in a good book.

Adam Longenbach received his Bachelor of Architecture from The Pennsylvania State University in 2010, his Master of Architecture, Theory History and Criticism from The Pennsylvania State University in 2011 and his Master of Architecture II, Urban Studies from Cooper Union in 2013. He is currently working in the New York City office of Snøhetta as a Researcher since 2015. Interests outside of architecture include the guitar, running and biking around Brooklyn, NY.

Rebecca Slocum received her Bachelor of Engineering from The Pennsylvania State University in 2014. After working for a few years as an engineer in the building industry she moved to England and is currently working on a Masters in Regional and Urban Planning at the London School of Economics and Political Science. She would like to pivot her career towards Urban Planning. Originally from upstate New York, Rebecca spent childhood summers in the Adirondack Park. She believes these formative years helped to inspire her interest in the built environment and propel her career ambitions today.

Reinhardt Swart received his Integrated Bachelor and Master of Architectural Engineering from The Pennsylvania State University in 2014. He has been working as an architectural lighting designer at SmithGroupJJR in Detroit, Michigan for the past three years. He is currently a member of the International Association of Lighting Designers, the Illuminating Engineering Society, and the AIA Detroit Committee on Diversity and Inclusion. His recent contribution to the General Motors Factory One project in Flint, Michigan helped win the 2018 AEI Professional Project Award in the Lighting Category. Outside of work, Reinhardt volunteers with Special Olympics of Michigan and with various community-based programs such as Forgotten Harvest, The Greening of Detroit, and Life Remodeled. His efforts extend to pro-bono work, providing lighting design services for the restoration of a local elementary school that will soon serve as a community learning center and co-working space. His other passions include music, art, art history, and philosophy.

Karalyn Slocum received her Bachelor of Science in Civil Engineering from The Pennsylvania State University in 2015, her Masters of Engineering in Environmental Engineering from The Pennsylvania State University in 2016. While in graduate school she worked closely with the Food, Energy, and Water research group and Penn State's ecological wastewater treatment facility and focused her studies in water quality chemistry and ecological treatment methods. She is currently a civil and environmental design engineer at Sasaki Associates in Boston, Massachusetts. Her passions remain tied to water and ecology and it continues to play a key role in her professional endeavors.

Lindsay Connelly received her Bachelor of Architecture and Master of Science in Architecture from The Pennsylvania State University in 2017. Her research examines contemporary funerary architecture's evolving social and cultural role in architectural practice and discourse. She currently practices architecture in Washington, D. C. She enjoys cooking, riding horses and visiting D.C.'s art museums.

Tena Pettit received her Bachelor and Masters in Architectural Engineering, specializing in Lighting + Electrical Option from The Pennsylvania State University in 2018. She currently works at Arup in their Lighting Design Studio in their Boston, Massachusetts office. Tena's passion for international development and sustainable design has taken her many places around the world and hopes this will continue to shape her future both personally and professionally. In her free time, Tena love to run, travel and explore new cultures and food, read, and spend time with her amazing family and friends.

CASE STUDY: DAVID MAPLE
U.S.-Mexico Border Wall

In time where technology and communication is creating a globalized-borderless economy, the United States is paradoxically isolating themselves through an increased border language. We must ask ourselves what agendas one may have for the creation of this wall.

To ensure reelection, politicians in today's government have come to rely on a practice of fear mongering with their consitituencies. By having the general public in a constant state of fear, politicians can advance their credibility by solving the public concerns and protecting them.

In the mid 1990s, politicians began using illegal drugs as a one sided debate which they knew they would draw no opposition. This tatic showed success in the reelection of President Clinton and today has created a model for political parties to expand into a variety of topics, including immigration reform.

From California to Massachusetts, politicians in the 2006 election founded their campaigns on protecting our borders and fighting illegal immigration, all the while knowing fully that the nation's economy could never survive without the labor class of undocumented workers.

By analyzing the political agendas, we can begin to understand a politician's motive and counter these arguments with the un-discussed effects these agendas have on the country's common pool resources.

By removing this labor class from our economic structure, resource systems such as agriculture will suffer. Even now, farmers are unable to find the necessary help to pick their fruit before rotting, leaving prices to soar as supply abruptly drops.

Rather than focusing on a single situation, this project takes a broad research approach which will prove the effects of a fortified the border.

Darla V. Lindberg

10 500 000 Unauthorized immigrants in the united states in 2005

1 085 395 Unauthorized immigrants deported in 2005 (total)

997 986 Unauthorized immigrants deported in 2005 who were unemployed

5 281 Unauthorized immigrants deported in 2005 who were employed

.4% Percent of unauthorized immigrants deported who were employed

$56 000 000 000 Dollars paid to medicare and social security by unauthorized immigrants

$0 Dollars in social security which will ever be paid to the unauthorized immigrant

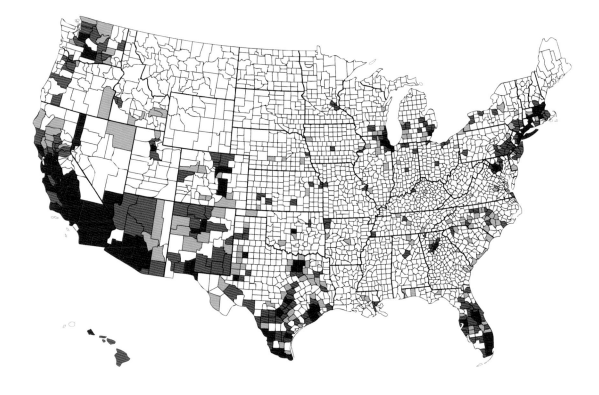

CASE STUDY: SARAH PETTIT
Property: Resource or Right?

Property: Resource or Right?
Privatization and Development in Northern
Liberties, Philadelphia
Sara Pettit, BArch 2009

Gentrification is an urban issue; one of community, of economics, of politics, and of disparity. As the city is a place of constant change and evolution, both in perception and form, cycles of influx and exodus define the very fabric of urbanity. Gentrification is simultaneously a stimulus and condition of such a cycle: as an urban node gains popularity by those outside of the group that causes this perceived desirability, those that are outside want in. If privatized development runs its course, the original inhabitants of the community find themselves displaced when the demand for the area increases the value of the supply. Thus, a city's response to issues of gentrification determines the degree of displacement and the methods of development. In a privatized method, development is unchecked by policy, and displacement will be high. On the other hand, if city investment is made, development can be healthy for the community, and the diversity of the urban fabric can be preserved.

Given that gentrification is part of the natural cycle of urban evolution and may have many positive effects on a community and its inhabitants, it is important that urban policy and infrastructure are capable of absorbing such change in a resilient fashion. An important aspect in reacting to gentrification in such a way is the encouragement, in policy and action, of healthy growth and improvement of the urban condition without resulting in displacement or further disparity in the human condition. Thus, in the case of the city Philadelphia, investment must be made in the gentrifying community of Northern Liberties and other developing areas to prevent over-privatization that results in displacement and loss of diversity.

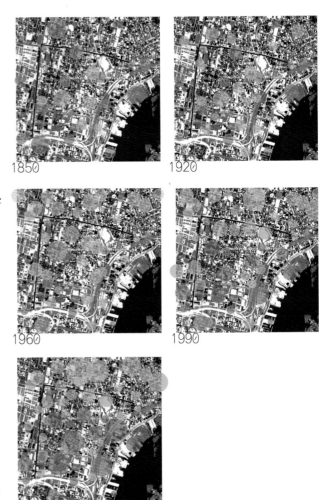

1850   1920

1960   1990

2000

CONSTITUTIONAL

At the constitutional level, we must look at the way that cities change and develop. This includes historical city changes and the waves of influx and exodus that define the very fabric of urbanity. In this sense, the policies regarding growth, zoning, and privatization come into play. Some cities employ regulations regarding public development within private, while some encourage the private as a means of financial gain, as seen in Philadelphia, and over-privatization results.

COLLECTIVE

The collective that is affected by the over-privatized development are the community members of Northern Liberties as well as the members of neighboring communities that feel the effects of th e development. Many existing residents are feeling pressure to relocate, and the neighborhoods to the north and west are also starting to feel some displacement pressure as the wave of gentrification continually moves in their direction. As the new development is of a homogeneous nature (trendy, expensive housing), the diversity that is the cornerstone of Northern Liberties is on the brink of extinction.

INSTITUTIONAL

The result is that Northern Liberties is becoming a closed community for those that cannot afford to live there. City policy and investment is ineffective in balancing the over-privatization that is overtaking the community. As there is no program to encourage cross-movement with surrounding communities (i.e. public + pragmatic space), Northern Liberties is more and more isolated within its larger context. Until policy helps to revive the diversity of the community, it will continue to slip further towards complete privatization and total loss of the public realm.

IN THE CASE OF NORTHERN LIBERTIES, THE EXISTING SITUATION IS BEST REPRESENTED BY GAME 04 - A HIGHLY INEFFICIENT SYSTEM OF OVERSEERS & PERSONAL INTERESTS THAT FAILS TO ADDRESS THE NEEDS OF THE COMMUNITY AT ALL SCALES. THE IDEAL GAME WOULD BE 05, RUN BY A SELF-FINANCED MULTIDISCIPLINARY OVERSEEING BOARD THAT IS INTERNAL TO THE COMMUNITY & IS COMPRISED OF REPRESENTATIVES OF THE PRIVATE DEVELOPERS, RESIDENTS, & THE CITY. BY INTERNALIZING THE OVERSIGHT PROCESS (NOW IN THE HANDS OF THE OVERBURDENED CITY OF PHILADELPHIA), DEVELOPMENT CAN OCCUR EFFICIENTLY & IN A WAY THAT ADDRESSES THE INTERESTS OF THE PRIVATE & PUBLIC SECTOR.

privatization

public strategy

CAPITALISM TAKES OVER. DEVELOPMENT IS UNCHECKED.

CAPITALISM CHECKED BY POLICY.

LOSS OF DIVERSITY [POPULATION, URBAN FABRIC, AND PROGRAM TYPOLOGIES] RESULTS.

GOVERNMENT MAINTAINS DIVERSITY THROUGH PUBLIC DEVELOPMENT

OVERABUNDANCE OF HOUSING, SATURATION OF THE HOUSING MARKET, INFLATION OF SALES PRICES AND TAXES

ENCOURAGEMENT OF PROGRAM VARIETY

RESULTS IN:

CLOSED COMMUNITY. ONLY OPEN TO THOSE THAT CAN AFFORD IT.

 V.

OPEN COMMUNITY. BALANCE OF WEALTH AND DIVERSITY IN ALL ASPECTS

NEIGHBORHOOD ASSOCIATION + PRIVATE DEVELOPER

P1 = PRIVATE DEVELOPER

P2 = NEIGHBORHOOD ASSOCIATION	COOPERATE	DEFECT
COOPERATE	IF BOTH THE COMMUNITY ASSOCIATION AND PRIVATE DEVELOPERS ELECT TO CO-OPERATE, THE RESULT WILL BE A BALANCED COMMUNITY. DEVELOPMENT WILL STILL HAVE SUBSTANTIAL ECONOMIC PAYBACK, YET THE NEEDS OF THE COMMUNITY WILL BE ADDRESSED, PROVIDED FOR, AND MAINTAINED. THUS, NORTHERN LIBERTIES WILL REMAIN DIVERSE AS DEVELOPMENT WILL ACCOUNT FOR INFRASTRUCTURAL AND CAPITALISTIC DEVELOPMENT.	IF THE NLNA COOPERATES IN ITS PART OF THE BARGAIN OF BALANCED DEVELOPMENT BUT THE PRIVATE DEVELOPER DEFECTS, OVER-PRIVATIZATION WILL OCCUR. AS A RESULT, PROPERTY VALUES WILL RISE UNCHECKED, AND DISPLACEMENT WILL RESULT FROM SUCH DEVELOPMENT. ADDITIONALLY, THE SOCIO-ECONOMIC, ARCHITECTURAL, AND PROGRAMMATIC DIVERSITY ARE THREATENED BY THE ECONOMIC MOTIVES OF THE PRIVATE SECTOR.
DEFECT	IF THE PRIVATE DEVELOPER COOPERATES WITH THE BALANCE OF DEVELOPMENT, YET THE NLNA DOES NOT HOLD UP ITS PART OF ENSURING COMMUNITY-MINDED PROJECTS, THEN THE BALANCE WILL STILL BE UPSET. PRIVATE DEVELOPMENT WILL OCCUR, BUT THE INFRASTRUCTURE AND PUBLIC PROJECTS, WHICH GIVE THE COMMUNITY INTERNAL STRENGTH, WILL NOT BE CARRIED OUT. THE RESULT WILL BE A WEAK COMMUNITY.	IF BOTH THE COMMUNITY ASSOCIATION AND PRIVATE DEVELOPERS ELECT TO DEFECT, THE RESULT WILL BE HIGH VACANCIES AND STAGNANT DEVELOPMENT. THERE WILL BE NO VALUE INCREASE OF PROPERTY IN THE COMMUNITY, AND THERE WILL ALSO BE NO BENEFIT FOR EITHER OF THE PLAYERS.

{let the games begin}

	COOPERATE	DEFECT
COOPERATE	10, 10	11, -1
DEFECT	-1, 11	0, 0

GAME 01 : PRISONER'S DILEMMA

In Game 01, the CPR is property in a developing community, and the players are private developers (P1) and existing residents (P2). If both cooperate, a balance will occur and both parties will benefit through economic payback and an improved community. However, the key to Game 01 is accepting that both groups have solely their self-interest in mind and thus lack organization and cohesion.

	COOPERATE	DEFECT
COOPERATE	10, 10	9, -1
DEFECT	-1, 9	-2, -2

GAME 02: CENTRAL AUTHORITY WITH COMPLETE INFORMATION

In Game 02, P1 is the private developer, and P2 is a community organization, a coalition of existing residents. In this game, the external authority is a City Development organization who enforces zoning rules and ensures fair development. The City officials have complete information and punish defections uniformly. The key to Game 02 is that the neighborhood association is a self-interested party that looks out for their own healthy development, allowing the city to invest less into overseeing the process.

	COOPERATE	DEFECT
COOPERATE	9.7, 9.7	8.3, -1.3
DEFECT	-1.3, 8.3	-1.7, -1.7

GAME 03: CENTRAL AUTHORITY WITHOUT COMPLETE INFORMATION

Game 03 has the same players and authority as Game 02; however, the City does not have complete information and therefore fails to punish defections uniformly. Defections are punished with the probability of y = .85, and cooperative actions with the probability of x = .15. Therefore, the players have more reason to defect, particularly in the case of the private developers. Because it requires more effort to correct defections, many issues would go unpunished due to improper oversight and action.

	COOPERATE	DEFECT
COOPERATE	9.2, 9.2	9.8, -1.8
DEFECT	-1.8, 9.8	-1.2, -1.2

GAME 04: CREATION OF EXTERNAL INSTITUTION

In reaction to the insufficiencies of enforcement in Game 03, a multidisciplinary development review board of residents, city agents, and private developers is created. As additional layers of oversight are added to the already lengthy and complicated process of development, the system may run less efficiently, although more fairly. The result is that defections are punished less uniformly than in game 03 with the probability of y = .6, and cooperative action with the probability of x = 4.

	COOPERATE	DEFECT
COOPERATE	10, 10	11, -1
DEFECT	-1, 11	0, 0

GAME 05 :SELF-FINANCED ENFORCEMENT

In Game 05, P1 and P2 make a contract that will be self-enforced, as each party has interest in the outcome. As an alternative to the two extremes of privatization and centralization, Game 05 is a sort of "eyes on the street" method of enforcement. A non-partial, external group could arbitrate to enforce the punishments that the players contractually agree to. This method is the most efficient with the CPR of property as it requires the least amount of exterior oversight. Most importantly, Game 05 addresses the reorganization of a city, allowing for feedback from smaller groups (neighborhoods) and give them means for organizing to have more power together.

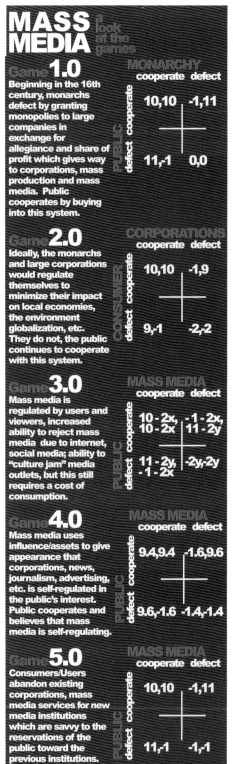

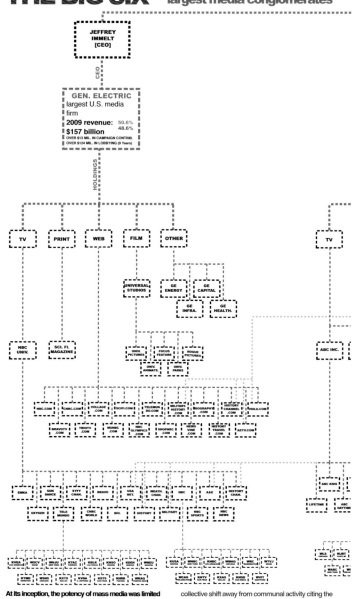

At its inception, the potency of mass media was limited to the few technologies available at that time. Gutenberg's invention of the printing press in 1441 allowed for advertising in newspapers, but few other means of corporate promotion were available until the invention of the radio and lithography and the automobile boom in the early 20th century leading to billboards and other signage. In fact, the term mass media was coined around the same time as these technologies bloomed. Today, society is subject to a multitude of mass media technologies from print to the television and the Internet, which are all accessible through a variety of other means.

In his book Bowling Alone, Robert Putnam discusses a collective shift away from communal activity citing the gradual decline and disbanding of social groups across the United States despite increases in popularity of the activities these groups were originally founded to promote. For example, and the title of the book, Putnam describes the rise in the number of people bowling over the last quarter of the 20th century while the number of bowling leagues and people joining them was on the decline. His research showed this trend of a percentage decline held true for every group ranging from the Kiwanis Club to the NAACP to the Parent-Teacher Association. Putnam also exposes the link between the exponential rise of mass media technologies in American households and the decline of community involvement.

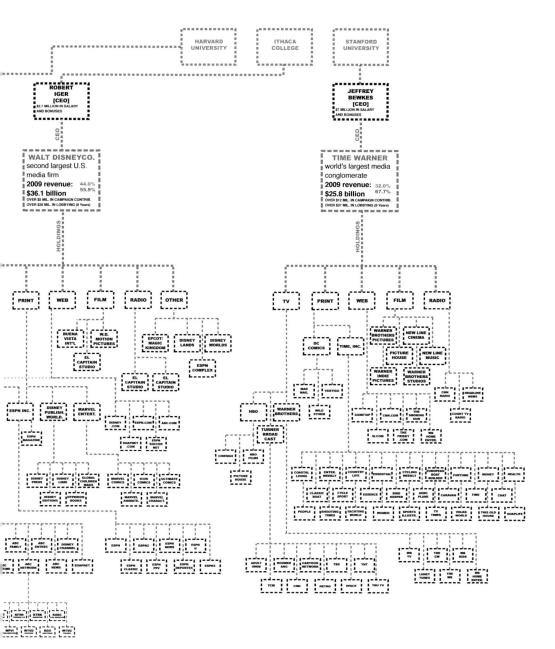

He describes the social consequences of mass media as follows: "No Longer must we coordinate our tastes and timing with others in order to enjoy the rarest culture or the most esoteric information. In 1900, music lovers needed to sit with scores of other people at fixed times listening to fixed programs, and if they lived in small towns as most Americans did, the music was likely to be supplied by enthusiastic local amateurs...In the last half of the century television and its offspring moved leisure into the privacy of our own homes". Furthermore, one third of all television watching is done alone, which means not only are families becoming isolated from one another, but members of a family are detached as well. Isolation is the bias of mass media, and the means by

which brands are communicated more effectively. An individual who is subjected only to a positive description of a product, a corporation's description unaltered by another person, is more likely to consume the product, and this is the scenario mass media allows corporations to create.

The polarizing effect of mass media is not unique to corporate advertising, but news organizations and politicians have grown savvy of its power as well. For example, in his book A Brief History of Neoliberalism, David Harvey cites Rupert Murdoch, CEO of News Corporation, as an example of media exploitation: "[Rupert Murdoch] is not above or outside particular

state powers, but by the same token he wields considerable influence via his media interests in politics in Britain, the US, and Australia. All 247 of the supposedly independent editors of his newspapers worldwide supported the US invasion of Iraq". Murdoch is certainly not alone in his description as a media exploiter as evidenced by the amount of money and resources media conglomerates expend to lobbying efforts and campaign contributions. As noted in the institutional mapping diagram above, General Electric, the largest media conglomerate, spent over 137 million dollars on political concerns from 1997 to 2006. 50.6% of their campaign contributions went to republicans and 48.6% went to democrats, though not all media conglomerates were split so evenly.

CASE STUDY: ADAM LONGENBACH
Deep-Rooted Institutions

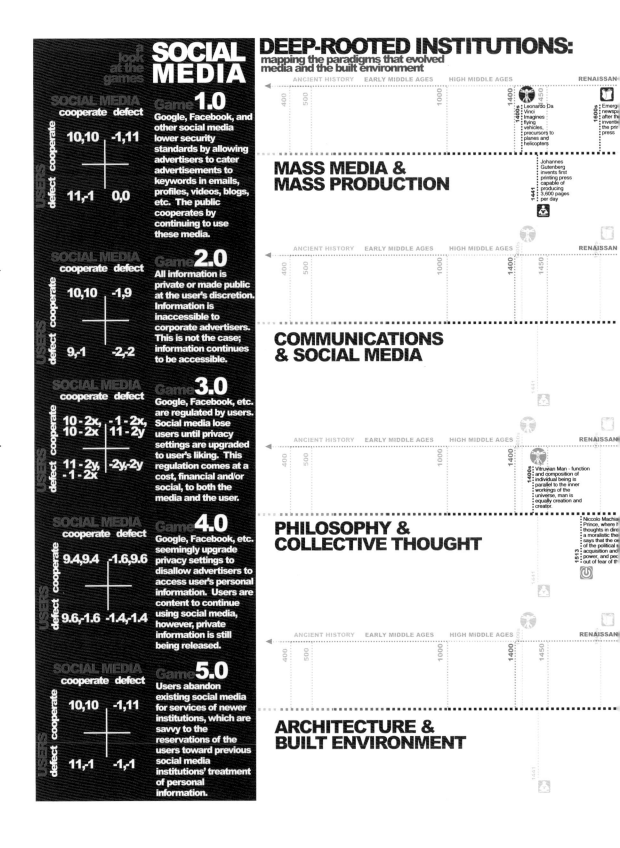

a look at the games

SOCIAL MEDIA

SOCIAL MEDIA — Game 1.0

	cooperate	defect
cooperate	10,10	-1,11
defect	11,-1	0,0

Google, Facebook, and other social media lower security standards by allowing advertisers to cater advertisements to keywords in emails, profiles, videos, blogs, etc. The public cooperates by continuing to use these media.

SOCIAL MEDIA — Game 2.0

	cooperate	defect
cooperate	10,10	-1,9
defect	9,-1	-2,-2

All information is private or made public at the user's discretion. Information is inaccessible to corporate advertisers. This is not the case; information continues to be accessible.

SOCIAL MEDIA — Game 3.0

	cooperate	defect
cooperate	10 - 2x, 10 - 2x	-1 - 2x, 11 - 2y
defect	11 - 2y, -1 - 2x	-2y,-2y

Google, Facebook, etc. are regulated by users. Social media lose users until privacy settings are upgraded to user's liking. This regulation comes at a cost, financial and/or social, to both the media and the user.

SOCIAL MEDIA — Game 4.0

	cooperate	defect
cooperate	9.4,9.4	-1.6,9.6
defect	9.6,-1.6	-1.4,-1.4

Google, Facebook, etc. seemingly upgrade privacy settings to disallow advertisers to access user's personal information. Users are content to continue using social media, however, private information is still being released.

SOCIAL MEDIA — Game 5.0

	cooperate	defect
cooperate	10,10	-1,11
defect	11,-1	-1,-1

Users abandon existing social media for services of newer institutions, which are savvy to the reservations of the users toward previous social media institutions' treatment of personal information.

DEEP-ROOTED INSTITUTIONS:
mapping the paradigms that evolved media and the built environment

ANCIENT HISTORY   EARLY MIDDLE AGES   HIGH MIDDLE AGES   RENAISSANCE

400   500   1000   1400 1450   1600s

Leonardo Da Vinci Imagines flying vehicles, precursors to planes and helicopters

Emerging newspaper after the invention of the printing press

MASS MEDIA & MASS PRODUCTION

Johannes Gutenberg invents first printing press capable of producing 3,600 pages per day
1441

COMMUNICATIONS & SOCIAL MEDIA

1441

PHILOSOPHY & COLLECTIVE THOUGHT

1400s Vitruvian Man - function and composition of individual being is parallel to the inner workings of the universe, man is equally creation and creator.

Niccolo Machiavelli Prince, where he thoughts in dire a moralistic the says that the o of the political acquisition and power, and peo out of fear of th
1513

ARCHITECTURE & BUILT ENVIRONMENT

1441

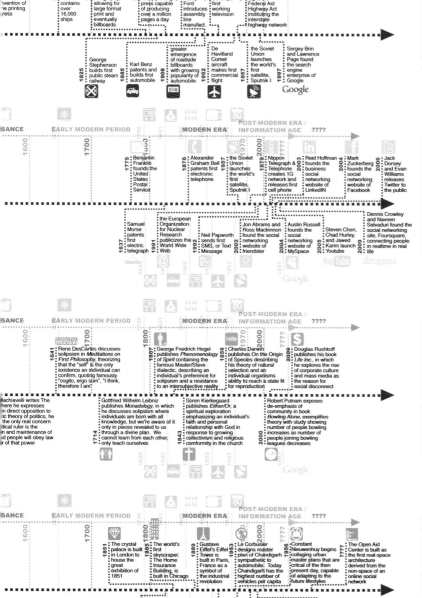

The emergence of the corporate structure paved the way for technologies of mass production that were biased to this breed of an economy. Corporate technologies helped to establish a framework for modern globalization. As fewer corporations began to mass-produce more goods for more people, it required a medium for connecting these people to the production, which is known today as mass media.

As the name suggests, the term social media is applied to media designed for social interaction through highly accessible means. Social media ties in with a long history of developing new technologies for person-to-person communication. Today, social media has grown to include Internet forums, social networking websites, social gaming, blogs, wikis, podcasts, pictures, video, etc. Most of which are accessible through new communication technologies such as smart phones.

The development of corporate and mass media social isolation was also a product of concurrent collective thought. As mass media developed, so too did paradigms concerning individuality and the self. Collective thought developing toward social and communal considerations as social media emerged may suggest the formation of a new paradigm concerning social integration with social media as a driving force. Social media is not a deterrent to face-to-face interaction, but a means of returning to face-to-face interaction.

Social isolation coupled with paradigms concerning individuality and the self were manifested in the built environment through isolated buildings, cities designed at the scale of the automobile rather than the human, suburbs and individual housing, etc. The new paradigm of social integration is only beginning to emerge in the built environment as post-industrial cities become more concerned with public space and web-based social networking sites require buildings to operate.

CASE STUDY: REBECCA SLOCUM
The Adirondack Park

The Adirondack Park of upstate New York encompasses six million acres. It is a combination of privately owned land and public forest preserves. Maintaining a balance between protecting the environment and nurturing an economy to sustain residents has been a major issue for the institution to deal with. Proceedings regarding a proposed development in the Park, The Adirondack Club have illuminated this struggle and exposed institutional flaws.

At the time of this writing in 2017, ground has not yet broken on The Adirondack Club project. Since talk about the project first began in 2004, the proposition has faced a myriad of trouble including multiple lawsuits. Plans for the resort include residential units, a hotel, marina, equestrian center and, the expansion and renovation of an old ski area on-site. Spread across 6,300 acres, the project is the largest development approved by the Adirondack Park Agency to date.

Real estate developers aim to profit off the pristine surroundings and existing tourist base in the area while environmental groups oppose the development. Other impacted parties include tourists, year-round residents, and seasonal residents. Ten million tourists visit the park each year. This group appreciates the natural scenery and benefits from development projects that provide additional recreation and lodging venues.

130,000 year-round residents reside in the park. This group is interested in protecting their beloved homeland, but wage serious concerns over economic decline and employment in the park.

110,000 seasonal residents enjoy their summer homes over vacations and weekends. This group's main concern is the preservation of pristine forest areas near their homes.

6 MILLION ACRES WHICH ENCOMPASS PUBLIC FORESTS PRESERVES AND PRIVATELY OWNED LAND. HOME
TO 100,000 ACRES OF OLD GROWTH FORESTS, 2,800 LAKES AND PONDS AND 1,500 MILES OF RIVERS[8].

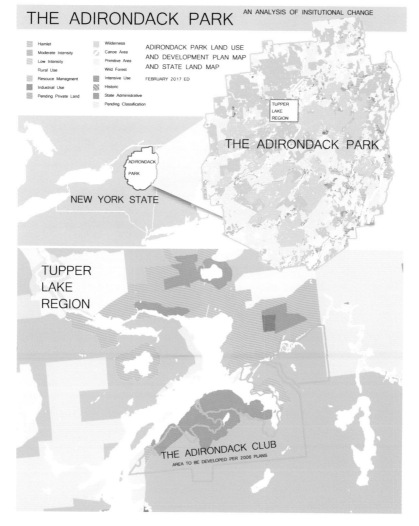

THE ADIRONDACK PARK

AN ANALYSIS OF INSITUTIONAL CHANGE

Hamlet
Moderate Intensity
Low Intensity
Rural Use
Resouce Managment
Industrial Use
Pending Private Land

Wilderness
Canoe Area
Primitive Area
Wild Forest
Intensive Use
Historic
State Administrative
Pending Classification

ADIRONDACK PARK LAND USE
AND DEVELOPMENT PLAN MAP
AND STATE LAND MAP

FEBRUARY 2017 ED

TUPPER
LAKE
REGION

THE ADIRONDACK PARK

ADIRONDACK
PARK

NEW YORK STATE

TUPPER
LAKE
REGION

THE ADIRONDACK CLUB

AREA TO BE DEVELOPED PER 2006 PLANS

Under constitution the environment has no rights, the family unit itself is biased so we create institutions.

GAME 1 1800s

The Adirondack Forest is a vast wilderness that has become a wealth of timber resources for developing New England towns and cities. In this matrix players are operating independently, consuming forest resources.

GAME 2 1885

The Forest Preserve is established by the State Legistalture over concerns about water and consumption of timber resources[1]. This land is to remain forever wild. The area is now protected and violators will be punished by the state.

GAME 3 1892

A state bill establishes the Adirondack Park. Encompassing 6 million acres the park is now comprised of public and private lands (including the original forest preserve)[1]. This compounds the protection set-forth in Game 2.

GAME 4 1971

The Adirondack Park Agency is instituted to to manage development in the park[1]. This provides additonal enforcement of park land.

GAME 5 1972+

Master Plans are approved. The State Land Map and Adirondack Land Use and Development Plan are now used by the APA to guide development in the park[1]. This results in a a dynamic community with rules that can be re-written over-time.

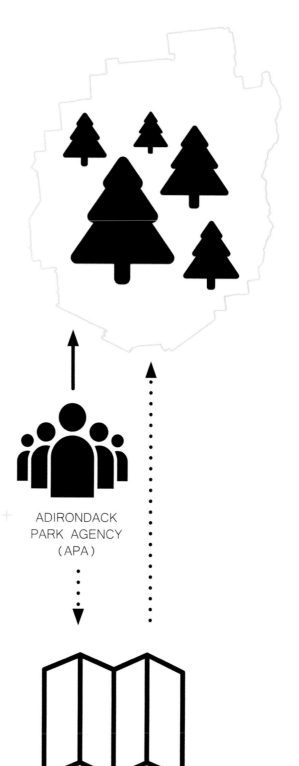

ADIRONDACK
PARK AGENCY
(APA)

Darla V. Lindberg

ENVIRONMENT
VERSES
ECONOMY

TIMELINE

2004 |||| 2012 ||| 2014 ||| 2014 ||| 2014 ||

Preserve Associates begins dealing with land owner[2]	APA approves permits to move the project forward[2]	Sierra Club & Protect the Adirondacks sue the APA, seeking to overturn the permits[2]	New York State's Supreme Cout Upholds the Permits[2]	Sierra Club's bid to appeal is rejected by the court[2]

YES   YES   NO

PLAYERS

ADIRONDACK   REAL ESTATE   ENVIRONMENTAL   SEASONAL
PARK AGENCY   DEVELOPERS   GROUPS   RESIDENTS
(APA)   (PRESERVE
                    ASSOCIATES)

‖2016 ‖2017 ‖2017 ‖‖‖‖‖ GAME 5 RETHINK

Legal filings
brought aginst
the project
over un-paid
bills[3]

Preserve
Associates pays
county back
taxes[3]

No ground
broken onsite

The Adirondack Club project pinned pro-development players against pro-environment players in a heated decade long stalemate. Both the shear size of the proposed development as well as environmental concerns appear to be its downfall.

It is the APA's responsibility to balance both the needs of the park and it's inhabitants. But, In the case of the Resort, Pro-environment players accused the Agency of supporting economic imperatives over the environment[4].

Vibrant communities are part of a stable park ecosystem. The solution to preventing further similar disputes lies in doing more to encourage development in the park's existing hamlets. These areas make up less than 1% of the park area. Year-Round Residents supported the Resort project out of desperation for employment opportunities. If more opportunity existed in the nearby hamlet of Tupper Lake, the Resort likely would not have felt local support. The state has taken strides to re-rehabilitate hamlets with its Hamlet Economic Planning and Assistance program. Moving forward, the APA needs to make a more concerted effort to support hamlet areas and educate local leaders, facilitating incremental development and economic prosperity.

YES   YES

YEAR-ROUND   TOURISTS
RESIDENTS

With the rise of digital technologies, today's growing sharing economy is an accepted form of transaction and spurs notable new human behaviors. Equity analyst at Brady Capital Research Inc., Barbara Gray, explains how the sharing economy (ex: Uber/AirBNB) provides under-utilized assets such as an empty car seat or spare bedroom that appreciates in value as both supply (i.e. drivers/hosts) and demand (riders/travelers) increase. Critical in this successful relationship is how human interaction and modern technologies facilitate trust and dual accountability – the monetary transaction seems almost secondary. Working rules are established and the cheat exposed: use social capital as a common-pool resource and provide services using today's advanced technological platform made possible in a connected network of accountable individuals.

Currently, we are experiencing Games 3/4, noted with a familiar theme in today's news –government-imposed regulations/limitations on services such as Uber and AirBNB so they abide by rules currently governing taxies and hotels respectively. Pressures from the prevailing economical model are attempting to regulate the sharing platforms in attempts to create a "fair playing field". While these efforts are somewhat justified, it may result in increased costs for current users of sharing services or in the case of Uber, more money taken from their drivers. Playing the Game out, I argue that true competiveness is possible; other people will find potentially better ways to work within the model of a sharing economy. The increasing popularity of Lyft, a direct competitor to Uber, reinforces this point. It follows that old-industries should re-think their business models instead of expanding imposed regulations; for example, taxi services using their own version of ride-hailing apps. I pause: at what point are these sharing economy start-ups "corporations" in-themselves? To what extent are regulations then effective?

Were Game 5 to be realized, I propose yet another cheat within ride-sharing platforms – autonomous vehicles. By introducing autonomous vehicles, the human aspects of mutual trust and accountability are diminished as we would interact with machines which are easily accessible through growing digital networks. As we speak, ride-sharing services are shifting their business models to work with the manufactures of these vehicles – for example, as of 2017, Volvo is to supply Uber with up to 24,000 self-driving cars – as their software alone will have little power in this new Game. In a similar manner, companies such as AirBNB are continuously adjusting their approach to their industry: in a 2017 interview with Fortune, Brian Chesky, CEO of AirBNB, notes: "I want to, in the next 10 years, get to this place where we can sell end-to-end trips...We will have created tens of millions of entrepreneurs who are creating experiences. A whole new part of the economy is the experience-based economy. And then we'll have also gone to aviation and started to redefine how we fly. Because what if flying was the best part of travel, not the worst part of travel? We call all this 'magical trips'—basically trips that are just amazing, memorable, end-to-end experiences." Both examples point to an ever-shifting sharing platform model, one that is also vulnerable to the next cheat.

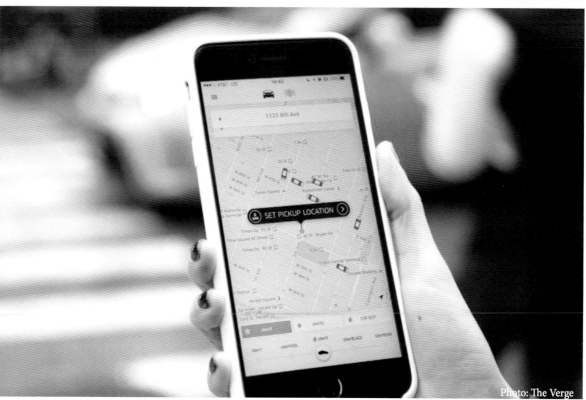

Photo: The Verge

AirBNB, founded in 2008, is valued at $31 billion as of 2017. AirBNB has processed 11 million resverations in 192 counties worldwide.

Photo: Airbnb
Source: CNBC

Uber, founded in 2009, is valued at $68 billion as of 2017. Uber now operates in over 500 cities in 72 countries.

Photo: Uber
Source: Wall Street Survivor

Source: DHL

 UBER **lyft** BREEZE wingz **JustPark**

 ⌂ **airbnb** HomeAway **wework**

 eb**ay** Etsy craigslist

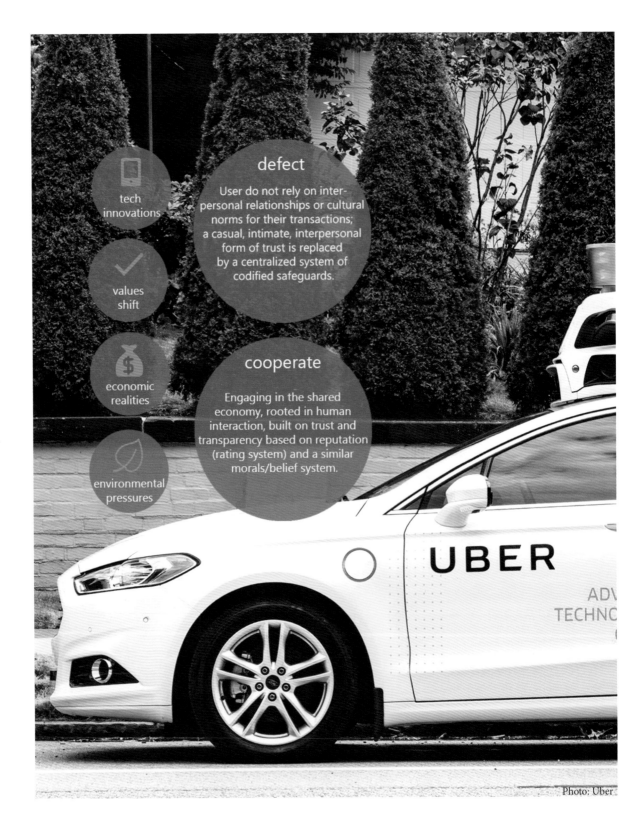

tech
innovations

values
shift

economic
realities

environmental
pressures

defect

User do not rely on interpersonal relationships or cultural
norms for their transactions;
a casual, intimate, interpersonal
form of trust is replaced
by a centralized system of
codified safeguards.

cooperate

Engaging in the shared
economy, rooted in human
interaction, built on trust and
transparency based on reputation
(rating system) and a similar
morals/belief system.

Photo: Uber

game 1 | expose the cheat

Increase public awareness of under-utilized personal assests, increasing our awareness of these extra resources. Uber, Airbnb, and the like create structural assets that appreciate in value as they attract more and more new hosts/drivers (i.e. supply) and travelers (i.e. demand) to their platform, leading to the ultimate network effect. Hereby, replace artificial institution trust with social capital by connecting supply and demand by capitalizing on filtering efficiency of social network reviews and facilitating trust through dual accountability systems.

game 2 | the ideal scenario

The idea that treating people well will result in a better experience. Act badly and you'll be barred from participating. Just like residents of pre-industrial America, sharing-economy participants know that every transaction contributes to a reputation that will follow them, potentially for the rest of their lives. New sharing economy companies are most likely to draw from a set of like-minded, forward-thinking early adopters. Invest trust in each other not corporations through peer-to-peer structure and accountability.

game 3 | the imperfect agent

Government places regulations on sharing economy. A valid concern follows that the sharing economy has the potential to undermine state activities through bypassing taxation. For example, Eric Schneiderman, New York State's attorney-general, demanded that Airbnb hand over records of its 15,000 hosts in NYC to verify that they pay taxes levied on hotels. Hosts will be much less likely to use a service if they're vulnerable to legal crackdowns. Even the fear of fines could push down housing supplies and dampen enthusiasm for Airbnb in its most important market. Simply, the government taxes "innovative ideas".

game 4 | the watcher of the watcher

Hotels and taxi companies holding courts and government accountable for laws: these laws are being imposed on them while not being imposed on sharing economy companies. For instance, taxi medallions are expensive. Uber drivers do not need medallions of licensed registration through NYC taxi services to be an employee of Uber. Moreover, cities such as New York City and San Fransisco are pushing to tax rooms rented to others through Airbnb. Exisiting landlords and residents complain of unfair advantages. Likewise, Airbnb is now seeing regulations that require the "leaser" to be present during the a guest's stay three-quarters of the time. Tim O' Reilly summarizes the evident growth of the sharing economy and disruption on exisiting corporations:

"The fact that regulators, tax collectors and big companies are now sniffing around a model that has been embraced by millions of people is a measure of its value and growth potential."

game 5 | revisiting the cheat

Open the market for competitiveness; this is emphasized by growing human behavior towards sharing economy. Other social apps will create competitive service at lower prices which begins the cycle of free-market economy, now on a sharing economic platform. Invest in each other not corporations through peer-to-peer structure and accountability. Examples include companies offering services similar to Uber (Hailo, Curb, Flywheel, and GetTaxi) and Airbnb (Hipmunk, Gogobot, Foursquare, and Hotel Tonight). "Uber's success and popularity should inspire legislators to take a hard look at the wasteful mass of ancient taxi regulations already on the books. Regulations were intended to protect consumers but now they block access to faster, more reliable service. Some people have designed a far more efficient system. Those medallions, licenses, and meters are obsolete. Admit it, and act accordingly." It follows that old industries should re-think their business models.

The fear in Game 5 is that a sharing economy will introduce less jobs (taxi drivers, hotel staff) and "less" economic spending. Further, privatization of Uber, for example, leads to more expensive services making room for other start-ups.

It should be noted that without governemnt intervention, an accepted cheat would be to go from Game 1 directly to Game 5. The sharing economies centralized trust infrastructures may catch obvious bad actors—purveyors of fake listings, money launderers, thieves—but it won't stop more run-of-the-mill offenders. That requires more subtle forms of social engineering: many companies are making up the rules as they go. "Central authority (government) can be positive if it facilitates to enhance the ability of local appropriators to engage in effective institutional design." (Ostrom)

As sharing economy platforms continuously adjust to advancing technologies and regulations, we can note new cheats resurfacing even within this established model (autonomous vehicles and experience-based trips).

Journey to Sustainable Aquaculture:

According to the FAO (Food and Agriculture Organization), aquaculture is the farming of aquatic organisms. This includes fish, mollusks, crustaceans, and aquatic plants.

Overfishing has led to the need of fish farms. In the last half century, 90% of large species, such as tuna and marin have been depleted due to over-fishing. On a global scale, about 32% of all fish stocks are overexploited or depleted. It has even been estimated that in 2048, we will not have any fishable species left. Alternate methods of fish production, known as aquaculture, is currently being used around the world to supplement for these loses.

Conventional fish farming produces almost half of the seafood eaten in the world, and that number is raising. The practice of convential fish farming grants private companie the right exploit public resources for financial benefit. The goal of creating a cheap and available food has resulted in the use of massive amounts of anti-biotics, hormones, pesticides, in overcrowded nets and strain on the environment. The current acceptableand practiced fish farming model is not sustainable for the growing industry.

However, sustainable aquaculture can be accomplished through a model that is able to manage change. Change in its environment, change in stake holder expectations, change in the market, and change in the world.

This case study focuses on the current problems with convential fish farming, highlighting stories of enviornmental devestation and human rights issues. It will then discuss a sustainable aquaculture model that values ecology and fulfills the eight design principals of a sucessful common pool resource institution.

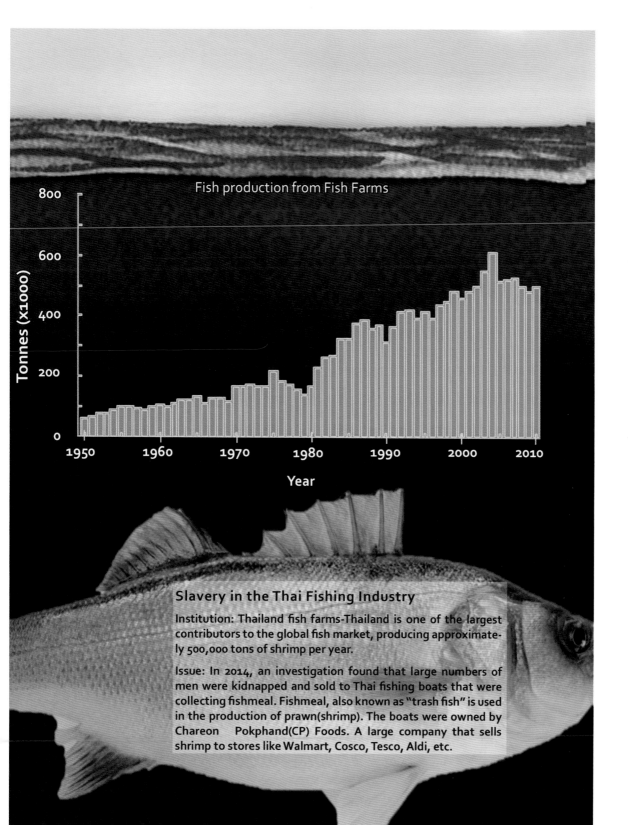

Fish production from Fish Farms

Slavery in the Thai Fishing Industry

Institution: Thailand fish farms-Thailand is one of the largest contributors to the global fish market, producing approximately 500,000 tons of shrimp per year.

Issue: In 2014, an investigation found that large numbers of men were kidnapped and sold to Thai fishing boats that were collecting fishmeal. Fishmeal, also known as "trash fish" is used in the production of prawn(shrimp). The boats were owned by Chareon Pokphand(CP) Foods. A large company that sells shrimp to stores like Walmart, Cosco, Tesco, Aldi, etc.

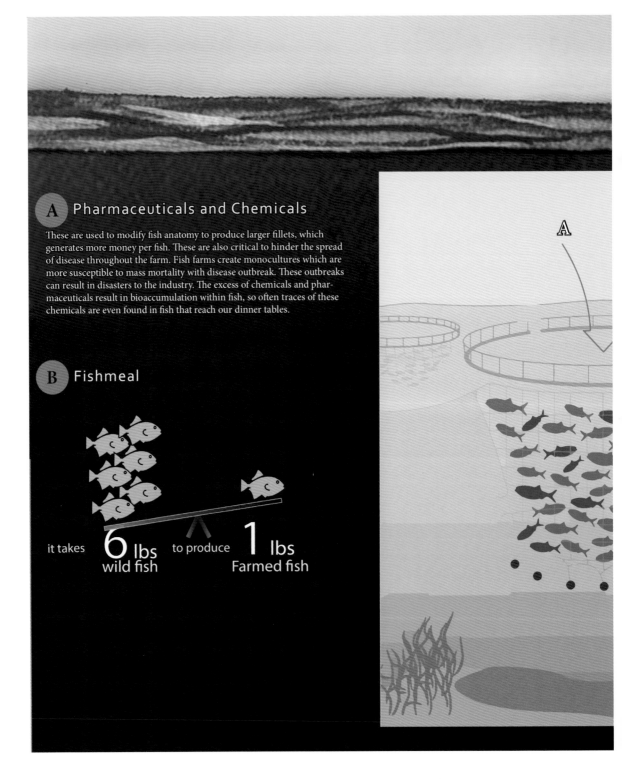

A Pharmaceuticals and Chemicals

These are used to modify fish anatomy to produce larger fillets, which generates more money per fish. These are also critical to hinder the spread of disease throughout the farm. Fish farms create monocultures which are more susceptible to mass mortality with disease outbreak. These outbreaks can result in disasters to the industry. The excess of chemicals and pharmaceuticals result in bioaccumulation within fish, so often traces of these chemicals are even found in fish that reach our dinner tables.

B Fishmeal

it takes **6 lbs** wild fish to produce **1 lbs** Farmed fish

A

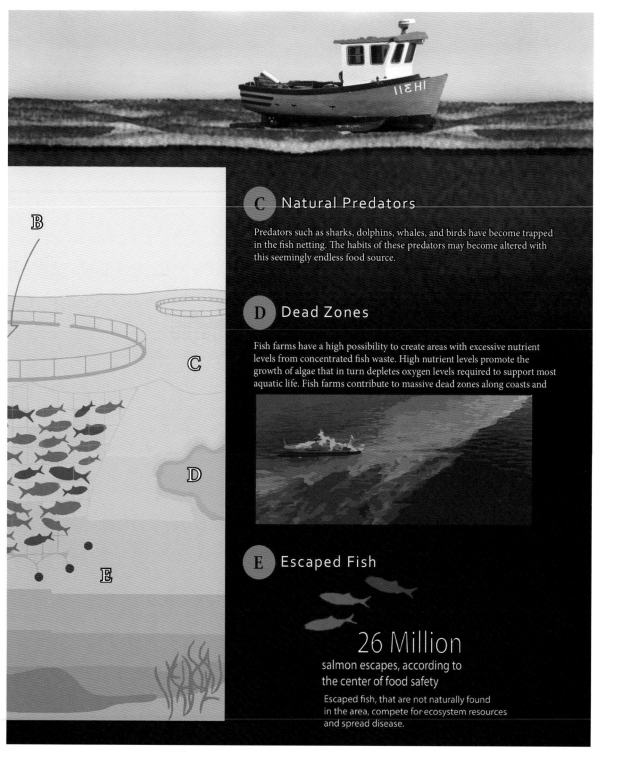

C Natural Predators

Predators such as sharks, dolphins, whales, and birds have become trapped in the fish netting. The habits of these predators may become altered with this seemingly endless food source.

D Dead Zones

Fish farms have a high possibility to create areas with excessive nutrient levels from concentrated fish waste. High nutrient levels promote the growth of algae that in turn depletes oxygen levels required to support most aquatic life. Fish farms contribute to massive dead zones along coasts and

E Escaped Fish

26 Million
salmon escapes, according to the center of food safety

Escaped fish, that are not naturally found in the area, compete for ecosystem resources and spread disease.

Veta la Palma | Sevilla, Spain

By rewriting the rules, sustainable aquaculture can be accomplished. Conventional aquaculture does not follow the 8 design principles discussed by Ostrom to sustain a successful Common Pool Resource Institution. The problems associated with the current institution are becoming more apparent as fish farming increases on a global scale. Veta la Palma is a fish farm in Southern Spain that has rewritten the rules and proving that sustainable aquaculture can be accomplished. Veta la Palma is a 3,200 hectare fish farm located at the mouth of two major rivers. The rivers provide a network of canals for drainage and 45 interconnected ponds. The natural wetland landscape and innovative engineering design creates and sustains a complex ecosystem. Veta la Palma produces 1,200 tons of sea bass, bream, red mullet, and shrimp each year for a major Spanish food conglomerate, Hisaparroz.

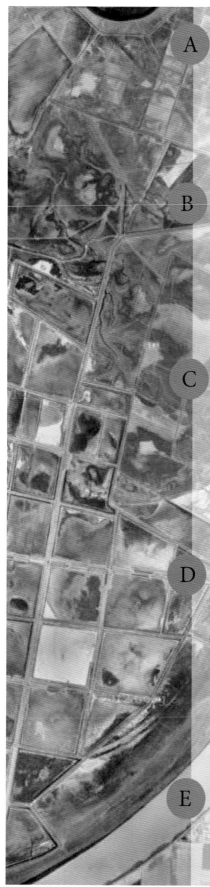

A Pharmaceuticals and Chemicals

The semi-open system allows for aquaculture diversity and the creation of a polyculture. Pharmaceuticals are not necessary to fight off disease that would wipe out an entire mono-culture fish farm. The farm is able to maintain its mission of sustainable and environmentally conscious production.

B Fishmeal

By creating an ecosystem and proper food chain, the farm does not require an outside source of fish protein or oils. Crustaceans and other aquatic invertebrates are produced year round and used as a source of a sustainable fish protein. In addition aquatic life, some land is also used to grow and keep cattle as alternate output food sources.

C Natural Predators

The success of fish production is measured by the number of predators that migrate to the area. In the case of Veta la Palma this success is accounted for in their bird population. There are over 250 species that populate Veta la Palma. Birds, like flamingos, use the land as a mating and feeding ground. The system is dependent on these birds, whose nests continue to sustain a successful wetland habitat.

D Dead Zones

This farm supports environmental services. The water that is used at Veta la Palma is returned to the river and ocean in excellent physical, chemical, and microbial quality. This is due to the constant flow of water through the system and the changes in salinity and nutrient concentrations. The positive growth of algae in the area allows the removal of nitrogen and phosphorus. The algae is a usable byproduct that can be used to make fish feed for non-carnivorous fish.

E Escaped Fish

The area is a natural estuary, one that supports inhabited fish and migratory fish species. An escaped fish would not disrupt the local ecosystem.

HART ISLAND AND THE HIGH COST OF DYING ALONE

Every year in the United States, thousands of people die alone, unclaimed, or unidentified. In most cases, people in these situations fall into the hands of the city or county they live in. The places they are finally laid to rest of often inaccessible, indecent places like Hart island, the largest tax funded cemetery in the world. Since 1898, over one million unclaimed and unidentified New Yorkers have been buried in unmarked, mass graves on Hart Island. To reduce costs to the tax payers, the burials are conducted by inmates from the nearby Rikers Island prison.

The people interred on Hart Island are not necessarily indigent or homeless, many people could not afford a private funeral or were not claimed by relatives within a month of death. Some people end up on the island simply because their family did not understand what they were signing when they agreed to a "city burial."

Hart Island erases the lives and stories of the people who are buried there. It is a physical result of the many chronic adversities of the human condition. It holds the harshest consequences of mental illness, addiction, and misfortune. While the island shrouds personal tragedies, it also obscures systematic failings that stack the odds against the most vulnerable individuals.

The common pool resource in this case study is access to a dignified death and adequate burial. This is both a natural and man-made resource system because being treated with dignity is a right we are ascribed at birth as humans, but the institutions, systems, and places we rely on for death and dying are man-made.

This situation is especially complex because of one group of appropriator's inability to speak up against the operational rules set by the institutions. Currently, the Department of Correction is both an appropriator and in charge of monitoring the conditions of the CPR it is involved with. Given that many of the individuals involved in the CRP cannot participate in modifying the rules or enforcing their efficacy or fairness, the DoC becomes an unregulated authority with no threat of sanctions for not following the rules of the CPR. This case study is a clear example of a situation that started without mutual monitoring – resulting in an absence of credible commitment or new rules proposed, and perpetuating undignified burials at Hart Island.

Darla V. Lindberg

261

THE POVERTY INDUSTRY:

Who is really benefitting from the current foreign aid model: the donors or the recipients?
How a seemingly benevolent, good hearted system has evolved into an industry driven by personal interests, incentives, and false assumptions.

The cycle of world poverty is due to a "broad tapestry" of norms, assumptions, and social and economic institutions that inhibit opportunities for under-resourced people to improve their situation. The current foreign aid industry exhibits no effect in eradicating poverty; in fact, it harms those in need even more. Weak institituions, bad policies, and a never ending economic, social, and political cycle within the impoverished communities and count make foreign aid often usless where it is most needed. The world often views the poor incorrectly; underlying assumptions and images make resource-restrained people appear hepless and dependent on foreign aid. They are viewed as objects of charity rather than people with their own unique stories. The poor are simply disconnected from global trade, lack legal protection and justice, and in many cases, are exploited by the broken paternalistic economic system and foreign influences through aid. Rising out of poverty and "climbing the ladder of prosperity" is possible. Communities need legal protection, a stable government without corruption, justice in the court system, land entitlement through the rule of law, and links to wider circles of business and world exchange. Unfortunately, there are incentives for donor governments, institutions, and people of great power to ensure that the poor cannot climb this "prosperity ladder" as their suffering is profitable to those on top. Who is really benefitting from the current foreign aid system?

THE PROBLEM

The current model for providing aid to the developing world does not work. Poverty can be approached as an industry in which those holding power in the system grow richer while those who need aid grow poorer. Incentives and motives for donor institutions to provide aid that benefits their needs combined with false information and assumptions about the recipient community and country's way of life, culture, and necessities perpetuate the cycle that is the poverty industry.

Taking a closer look at the operation behind the World Bank and International Monetary Fund (IMF) exposes how eliminating poverty could destroy an entire profittable industry and those in positions of power. When giving loans to developing countries, there are several "conditionalities" placed on the borrowing countries by the World Bank and IMF without much considerations in regards to the individual economic circumstances or needs of the people. To receive the loans, the recipient country must essentially restructure its economic system in accordance with that recommended by the World Bank and IMF. Eliminating a country's economic freedom in decision making removes all incentive for them to grow and develop independently and in ways that would benefit their personalized needs. False assumptions and incorrect knowledge about what a community really needs to succeed cannot be determined by an outsider structuring the loans. Rich and powerful institutions with their own adgendas re-designing the economic structure of these vulnerable communities and countries is the ideal set-up for donors to profit on the backs of the poor. The IMF forces local small businesses and farmers in the recipient countries to shift production of goods originally for local consumption to production of cheap exports to wealthy countries, undermining the local market. The wealthy donor countries receiving the cheap imports are also encouraged to give tax breaks and subsidies on the products, further devaluing the developing country's goods. As the local industries are destroyed by these policies, large multinational corporations arrive, often exploiting local workers with terrible wages and working conditions and with little concern for their environment. The local economy cannot compete or even survive with the intervention of the donor institutions. Without economic prosperity, the poor remain poor and the rich profit from their own "aid". In addition, many projects funded by the World Bank often have negative social and environmental implications for the developing communities - large infrastruture projects have been designed and implemeted with little to no knowledge in regards to the local environment, culture, or people. These "helpful" projects result in negative effects for the environment and often displace large numbers of people.

The donor loans from the World Bank and IMF must eventually be repaid by the community and country in need. To repay these enormous depts, the people must often cut spending on education and health care, eliminate food and transportation subsidies, devalue their currency to make exports cheaper, and privatize necessary state institutions. The recipient country becomes an economic slave to these donor loans originally designed to help escape poverty. The influence of the World Bank and IMF lower the already suffering standard of living of the poor people in need.

Such a system also provides the perfect breeding ground for corrupt leaders to rise in these poverity-stricken communities and countries. For the elite in the developing countries, they are often convinced the only solution is the continual influx of foreign aid, forever perpetuating the current aid instury and continually devastating the communities in poverty.

THE CURRENT SYSTEM

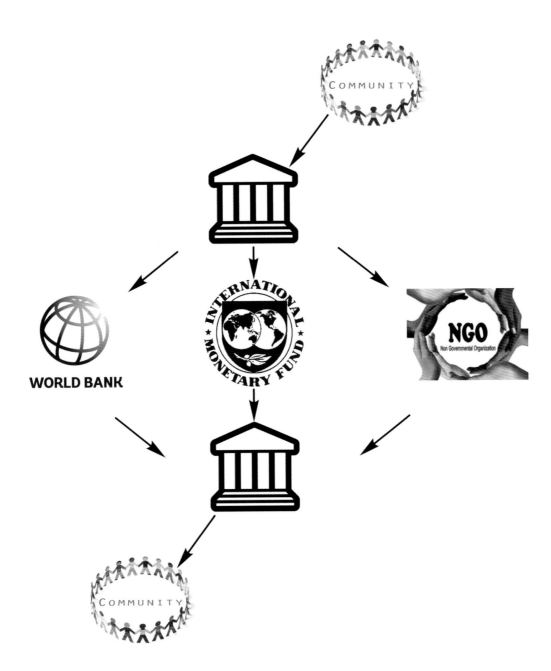

THE PLAYERS

WORLD BANK

donor: THE WORLD BANK

The World bank is an international financial institution that provides loans to developing countries for capital programs. The organization's official stated goal is reducing global poverty. All decisions in regads to loans given and projects funded by the World Bank must be guided by a commitment to promote foreign investment and international trade as well as facilitating Capital Investment. First formed after World War II to provide aid in rebuilding war-torn Europe, the World Bank's success in that mission translated into the model for providing aid to the developing world.

donor: THE INTERNATIONAL MONETARY FUND [IMF]

The International Monetary Fund [IMF] is an international organization of 189 countries that work together to "foster global monetary cooperation, secure financial stability, facilitate international trade, promote high employment and sustainable economic growth, and reduce poverty around the world." The IMF is funded with taxpayer dollars from the 189 countries in agreement. However, the IMF's structure in affluent countries dominate voting power and decision making does not allow the input from the poorest and most affected and impoverished communities in designing loans. Such disproportion of power allows the personal interests of politicians, stakeholders, bankers, investors, and corporations of the wealthy donor countries to act in self-interest with their own personal agendas placed ahead of the poor.

donor: NON-GOVERNMENT ORGANIZATIONS [NGOs]

Non-government organizations, or NGOs, are "private organizations that pursue activities to relieve suffering, promote the interests of the poor, protect the environment, provide basic social services, or undetake community development." NGOs receive funding from charitable donations and volunteer service. Unfortunately, large subsidies are given to NGOs who do work in such countries: the people in leadership positions in the organizations can end up making large, tax free profits. Other aid agencies, charities, and social entrepreneurs have similar models and effects of those of NGOs.

recipient: DEVELOPING COUNTRIES & COMMUNITIES

The critieria for defining a developing country include people having a lower life expectancy, less education and lower literacy rates, lower incomes, and women having higher fertility and pregnancy rates.

All images obtained from Global Brigades, the largest student run sustainable development and global health organization. [www.globalbgrigages.org]

THE GAMES

game ONE: the defection

The current foreign aid model is not only ineffective in solving world poverty, but also severely detrimental for the developing recipient countries. Self-motivated donor organizations and false assumptions about developing countries and their needs fuels the continuation of the poverty industry. The poor are viewed as objects of profit rather than people with individualistic needs. The recipient developing countries and their economies suffer from the policies placed on them from the donor aid institutions, perpetuating the cycle of poverty.

game TWO: the ideal scenario

The donor and the recipient players working together in cooperation and collaboration could result in the eradication of global poverty. Rather than aid flowing from player to player in the system which acts under a veil of secrecy and with little understanding in regards to where the aid is allocated or what services it provides to those in need, there would be direct communication about aid distribution between all parties involved. Instead of self-interests driving the decisions and policies of donor institutions, the needs of the poor would determine aid distribution. Sweeping generalizations and assumptions about the recipient communities would be replaced with a plan presented by the community members themselves. An external agent unattached from any political, social, and economic self-interested motives from either party would monitor the system, ensuring corruption would not occur.

game THREE: the reality

The parties involved cannot act perfectly and the players do not always act with the proper intentions. Greed for economic power and monetary gains by the World Bank, IMF, and NGOs often overshadows the needs of the poor; taking advantage of the vulnerability and disconnectedness of the impoverished can be simple. Ignorance in regards to the needs of communities also hinders the success of foreign aid. An agent cannot perfectly monitor all those interacting in this system; any external agent may gloss over the actions of one party, harming the system.

game FOUR: the appended

It is difficult for an external agent to remain partial and unbiased from either side. The donor institutions and recipients in the system must monitor the intentions, assumptions, and actions of one another. Each player should have an advocate representing and communicating with the others. It is most important that the developing countries in need are present and their voices heard.

game FIVE: the empowerment

Rather than the current foreign aid system acting top-down, small grassroots movements emerging bottom-up from the communities themselves is the only solution to eliminating poverty. Any foreign aid distribution must be used to mobilize partnership with communities and those providing aid rather than the paternalistic method from donor institutions that is currently in use. The people of the community must be empowered through education, training, and entrepreneurial connections to the global market. It is the duty of donor institutions and those in power to set aside their own personal agendas, listen to the people of the impoverished communities, and work collaboratively, empowering one another, eliminating poverty together. "Give a man a fish and you feed him for a day; teach a man to fish and you feed him for a lifetime."

CONCLUSION

Russell Ackoff, Professor Emeritus of The Wharton School, was affectionately known as the "Einstein of Problem Solving." Ackoff idealized design and design thinking. According to Ackoff, architects are natural systems thinkers. They never think of a room separate from the entire building or the building separate from its entire context. In design, the larger decisions affect the smaller ones and vice versa. Social theorists play an essential role by stepping *outside of the skin* of a subject to consider the larger and longer bearing of our collective knowledge domains. My own work is inspired by designers who wear multiple hats and challenge the status quo. William Morris and his contemporaries in the 1800s are one of many to work this way. Morris, a poet, philosopher, typographer, political theorist, along with Philip Webb, John Ruskin, A.W. N. Pugin, Pevsner, to name only a few from the Arts and Crafts movement are influential figures who questioned the effects of industrialization on design, traditional craft, the social wellbeing of a city and of life in general. They worked as vigorously to contest the effects of urban sprawl and the treatment of the poor as they did to exemplify how the social and moral health of a nation was expressed in the nature of its architecture and in the manner of its work. I'm also encouraged by the daring and pioneering efforts in Biomimicry. Scientists, chemists, engineers, all learning from one another looking to Nature's processes, principles and properties to inform new ways of working and building and living together. In this book, I organized powerful social influencers from three distinct properties of systems behaviors—indeterminacy, synchronicity and doubt—citing examples from the arts, science and humanities. I referenced the Social Contract Theory and used Game Theory to illustrate how we create social suckers of cooperating individuals—those who would like to leave their children a better planet than what they inherited—and how innovation is possible because we've built sloppy institutions. And, yet, an innovative application of Elinor Ostrom's game theory games demonstrates the layering of inefficient bureaucracy hinders the ability of grassroots initiative and more effective governmental regulation to safeguard essential Commons ecosystems and economies. I lobby for a new way of writing and recalling history to include a systems-wide knowledge domain with emphasis on an awareness of major generational "blind spots" in institutional memory causing disruptions such as Enron to flatline economies and destroy vulnerable ecologies. These are not market checks and balances, as we are often taught to believe. Following the Money, we see instead, it's how the gap widens between the Haves and the Have-Nots. I consider the Strauss-Howe generational influencers with the *Theory of Cycles* and look more closely at the 20-year phase of life between 35 and 55 when individuals are most likely to move into positions of leadership. I, then, overlay that influential 20-year life phase with historic charts tracking crop yields by Samuel Benner in the 1800s and adapted to economic markets by A. J. Frost in the 1900s. I then extended those patterns on to the present charts used by asset managers managing our retirements, consistently mapping the 16 + 18 + 20 year economic fluctuations in market highs, recessions and panics. According to Strauss-Howe, the Millennials Generation (1982-2004) was shaped by unraveling cultural wars. Those born in 1982 became 35 in 2017. Millennial "Digital Natives" born after 1992 (the Internet and Social Media) will be 35 in 2027. The Homeland Generation (2005-present) have been shaped by a Great Recession/War on Terror/ Sustainability. Homelanders born in 2005 will be 35 in 2040. Projecting Benner's, Frost's and current asset management cycles using 16 + 18 + 20 year (54 year total) projections reveal a major panic in 2021 (when Millennials turn 35 and Baby Boomers are retiring) and another in 2041 (when Homelanders turn 35). Extending the 16 + 18 + 20 year cycle through the '80s to the 2001 Enron Crisis to today, we are witnessing a repeat cycle of political influence to deregulate banks and erode environmental policy into 2021. So, we ask, "what kind of leaders will the Millennials or the Homeland Generation be when they reach the influential age of 35 to 55 in these (potentially) critical times of market panic?" A recent article in *Politico* magazine titled, "My Generation Is Never Going to Have That," by Paul Roberts (April 26, 2018), openly challenges housing development and neighborhood zoning that biases the traditional single family home of the Baby Boomer generation, now, financially out of reach for even the best-paid young person entering the workforce. Millennials, currently the largest demographic in the country, who previously considered themselves apolitical, find they have a role to play as activists fighting for more neighbors, not less. Data miners are making a case for middle-class families and young graduates to share in the wealth and equity of home ownership. Finally, urban transformers feel a moral imperative in taking on the social, economic and environmental reform of the city befitting of future generations equipped to take on some of Society's larger structural issues. The Case Study Contributors are exactly this demographic and their proposals show courageous and pioneering approaches that are neither insignificant or insurmountable.

CONCLUSION

Darla V. Lindberg

273

POSTSCRIPT

In the beginning I said this wasn't a book about politics, money or religion. I also said it was a book about how to extract a theory from a milieu in order to design enlightened architecture, inform designers and engage citizens. I can't finish without reflecting on the reality that I worked 30 years to put this material together only to be writing it in a time when this material seems to be growing more and more essential. But our time is marked by larger systems that aren't quite visible to us today. My intention is to write for those more optimistic times well into the future—*to plant acorns knowing we will never live to harvest the oaks*. Whenever someone asks me to describe a systems approach to thinking about design, I use this illustration. It's about a sculptor who goes up into the Wasatch mountain range and studies a section of rock for every evidence revealing the characteristics of the granite deep inside. He considers the terrain to see how the water is channeled. Vegetation tells him something about the roots that will make cuts into the earth exposing surfaces for centuries of erosion. After much inspection, he extracts a section to bring down to his studio. He spends more time with the rock, reading the clues, relying on information foreign and familiar to him. Eventually, he takes a chisel and hammer and makes a deliberate cut. If he is right, and all the systems align, the cut reveals a perfectly smooth face of granite deep inside the rock. If he's wrong, the effort results in rubble. Exaggerated, or not, the illustration reminds us to be patient, and look *Outside the Skin* to reveal deeper mysteries within.

I was an architecture student traveling abroad in 1977 when the Centre Pompidou opened. I thought it was genius. Designed by competition winners Richard Rogers, Renzo Piano with Gianfranco Franchini, and assisted by Ove Arup & Partners, the Centre was inspired to be a multicultural complex bringing together different forms of art and literature as well as public markets and entertainment.[136] It included several significant cultural centers—the Bibliotheque publique d'information (a vast public library), the Musee National d'Art Moderne (largest museum of modern art in Europe), and a center for music and acoustic research.[137] The complex with its expressed mechanical, electrical, circulation and fire safety systems "revolutionised museums, transforming what had once been elite monuments into popular places of social and cultural exchange, woven into the heart of the city." Building on the radical architecture conceptualized at the time by the "apolitical and antigravitational pop graphics"[138] of Archigram (Plug-in City),[139] Cedric Price and Joan Littlewood (Fun Palace),[140] Rogers and Piano imagined a "factory of culture." Forty years later, the Pompidou is still one of the most optimistic icons of the 20th century, "an accidental monument that became a symbol of a radical and optimistic time."[141] A perfect example of the part-to-the-whole, the Pompidou is a story told, like the building itself, "piece by piece," in a composition instantly the "unexpected trip"[142] of the time.

I started my book by thinking back on the L.A. Riots of 1992 and how the thinkers and architects in that city created their own thoughtful response to the messy milieu confronting them. Fifteen years earlier, the architects and engineers of the Centre Pompidou were doing the same. Reyner Banham said of the Centre at the time of its opening, "Not many outside the charmed circle of modern architecture have even heard of Archigram and of its apocalyptic struggles in an unresponsive society."[143] Only the Centre Pompidou stood as a reminder that the milieu may not be fully understood until, *maybe*, 40 years later.

Radical ideas triggering some of history's most innovative solutions in any domain often come from an iridescent thought by a single person. But then, any game-changing thinker will tell you those ideas come from a bundling of often random, relevant, and non-linear threads of information, conversations, research, and experiences to render that single brilliant point-of-departure. Being curious about everything, especially processes and approaches, seemingly well outside the domain and the particulars of any one problem, is a common characteristic of a systems thinker. Then real solutions evolve in a similar fashion. The list of projects needing brilliant (even not-so brilliant) Commons solutions are endless. And outside of academia and disciplinary divisions, they all share the need for the entire village thinking and working together. Consider the innovator turning waste plastic into roads and highways relieving landfill and lasting longer than concrete. A single suggestion to redistrict water rights according to the protection of essential underground aquafers and resources seems embarrassingly simple when we compare it to the endless stories of communities battling through exhaustive litigation based on property ownership and state lines. I'm currently tracking the story of the Gateway tunnel project between New Jersey and New York. Currently estimated at $11 billion and carrying 200,000 daily passengers under the Hudson River, an engineering marvel to save Gotham and the entire North East corridor from disaster is the kind of megaproject today that would rival the Dam project bringing electricity and water to the expanding South West in the early '30s. The Hoover Dam is still considered one of humanity's proudest moments. Still, while these megaprojects tell a story about our milieu, underlying all of society's larger structural issues are political battles. Critical projects become pawns for politicians in power. Yet, if you study these projects from the distance of time, the bright spot is politicians come and go. Politics seem huge in the moment and their impact can affect a generation or longer. The temporary stall they create often leads to better solutions in the long run. Protests, the foot march, and frown power become key forces for mobilizing decisive moments and influencing a next generation of influencers. Innovators currently building comparable tunnel and infrastructure projects in Paris and around the world offer solutions that lower the costs of construction making it possible to spread budget allocations to other infrastructure projects and public transit affecting urbanism well beyond Manhattan today. To this end, the key to solving society's larger structural issues today is to weave together the work of a courageous many operating in think tanks or industry, private and non-profit enterprises, advancing everything from politics to resources constructing a new kind of awareness. History written by mapping the big picture, the long story, the short strategy, and including the array of players, events, stakeholders, and influencers contributes to the characterization of the milieu. Design solutions intent on capturing this larger story teach us not only how to be aware of our time as one slice of a continuum, but also, to own a place in that continuum by contributing to the longer inclusive story. The lessons learned by unpacking systems-wide events like Enron's story, or the Benner and Frost cycles, or tracking a project like the Gateway project teach us one Wall Street meltdown, one seasonal crop cycle, one tunnel may not be a game changer, but learning how not to break the bank or destroy the planet would be.

ENDNOTES

PREFACE

Figure 1. Yellow Pages
Figure 2. Fairness Framework
Figure 3. Twenty-Year Lag
Figure 4. LA riots

1 Ostrom, E. (1990). *Governing the commons: The evolution of institutions for collective action* (Political economy of institutions and decisions). Cambridge; New York: Cambridge University Press.

2 Burke, E., & Ritchie, D. (1992). *Further reflections on the revolution in France*. Indianapolis: Liberty Fund.

3 Saraiya, S. (2017). The 1992 L.A. Riots, a Quarter-Century Later. *Variety*, 335(14), 133.

4 Twomey, J. (2004). SEARCHING FOR A LEGACY: THE LOS ANGELES TIMES, COLLECTIVE MEMORY AND THE 10TH ANNIVERSARY OF THE 1992 L.A. "RIOTS'. *Race, Gender & Class*, 11(1), 75.

5 "Los Angeles Riots, 1992 (1)," (https://www.youtube.com/watch?v=P43W Zd611WA).

6 Morgan, & Morgan, Morris Hicky. (1960). *Vitruvius: The ten books on architecture*. New York: Dover Publications.

INTRODUCTION

7 Porter, Kak, Porter, William A, & Kak, Subhash. (1989). *Advances in communications and signal process ing* (Lecture Notes in control and information sci ences;129). Berlin; New York: Springer-Verlag.

8 Bertalanffy, L. (1969). *General system theory; foundations, development, applications*. New York: George Braziller.

9 "Buckminster Fuller Institute," (https://www.bfi.org/).

10 Fuller, R. (1983). *Inventions* (1st ed.). New York:
St. Martin's Press.

11 Ibid, (https://www.bfi.org/).

12 Bertalanffy, L., & LaViolette, P. (1981). *A systems view of man*. Boulder, Colo.: Westview.

13 Boulding, K., Dolfsma, W., & Kesting, S. (2013). *Interdisciplinary economics Kenneth E. Boulding's engagement in the sciences* (Routledge Studies in the History of Economics). Abingdon [England]: Rout ledge.

14 Chapanis, A. (1958). An Introduction to Cybernetics.
W. Ross Ashby. *The Quarterly Review of Biology*, 33(1), 97.

15 Gideon. (n.d.). Chadwyck-Healey.

16 Elliott, C. (1992). *Technics and architecture: The development of materials and systems for buildings*. Cambridge, Mass.: MIT Press.

17 Stichweh, R. (2000). Systems theory as an alternative to action theory?; the rise of 'communication' as a theoretical option. *Acta Sociologica*, 43, 5-13.

18 Parsons, T. (1977). *Social systems and the evolution of ac tion theory*. New York: Free Press.

19 Luhmann, N., & Barrett, R. (2012). *Theory of society Volume 1* (Cultural memory in the present). Stanford, Calif.: Stanford University Press.

20 Ludwig von Bertalanffy – General Systems Theory – 1950, (http://www.nwlink.com/~donclark/history_isd/bertalanffy.html).

21 Banathy, B., & Jenlink, P. (2005). *Dialogue as a Means of Collective Communication*.

22 Parsons, T. (1978). *Action theory and the human condition*. New York: Free Press.
Parsons, T. (1969). *Politics and social structure*. New York: Free Press.

23 Odum, H. (2007). *Environment, power, and society for the twenty-first century the hierarchy of energy* (New ed.). New York; Chichester: Columbia University Press.

24 Odum, E. (1993). Ecology and our endangered life-support systems (2nd ed.). Sunderland, Mass.: Sinauer Associates.

25 Capra, F. (1996). *The web of life: A new scientific understanding of living systems* (1st Anchor Books ed.). New York: Anchor Books.

26 Senge, P. (1999). *The Dance of change: The challenges of sustaining momentum in learning organizations* (1st ed.). New York: Currency/Doubleday.

27 Swanson, R. (2010). Foundations of Human-resource Development (2nd ed.). *Human Resource Management International Digest*, 18(7), 142-144.

28 "The California State University," (https://fresca.calstate.edu/faculty/2545).

29 Prigogine, I. (1980). *From being to becoming: Time and complexity in the physical sciences.* San Francisco: W. H. Freeman.

30 Maturana, H., & Varela, F. (1980). *Autopoiesis and cognition: The realization of the living* (Boston studies in the philosophy of science; v. 42). Dordrecht, Hol land; Boston: D. Reidel Pub.

31 Ackoff, R. (1999). *Re-creating the corporation a design of organizations for the 21st century.* New York: Ox ford University Press.

32 Bajcsy, R. (2010). Ubiquity symposium "What is computation?": Computation and informa-tion. *Ubiquity*, 2010(December), Ubiquity, 01 Decem ber 2010, Vol.2010(December).

33 Banathy, B. (1996). *Designing social systems in a changing world* (Contemporary systems thinking). New York: Plenum Press.

34 Nechansky, H. (2010). The relationship between: Miller's living systems theory and Beer's viabile systems theory. *Systems Research and Behavioral Science*, 27(1), 97-112.

35 Checkland, P. (1999). *Systems thinking, systems practice* (New ed.). Chichester, England; New York; John Wiley.

36 Sarne, D., & Grosz, B. (2013). Determining the value of information for collaborative multi-agent planning. *Autonomous Agents and Multi-Agent Systems*, 26(3), 456-496.

37 Flood, R. (2017). Thirty Years of Systemic Practice and Action Research. *Systemic Practice and Action Research*, 30(3), 209-211.

38 Leonard, A. (2015). Stafford Beer and the legacy of Cybersyn: Seeing around corners. *Kybernetes,* 44(6/7), 926-934.

39 Napp, N., & Nagpal, R. (2014). Distributed amorphous ramp construction in unstructured environments. 32(2), 279-290.

40 Capra, F. (1982). *The turning point: Science, society, and the rising culture*. New York: Simon and Schuster.

41 Blum, M. (2016). Cybernetics: A mathematician of mind. *Nature*, 538(7623), 39-40.

42 Prietula, Carley, Gasser, Prietula, Michael J, Carley, Kathleen M, & Gasser, Leslie George. (1998). *Simulating organizations: Computational models of institutions and groups.* Menlo Park, CA: AAAI Press/MIT Press.

43 Jackson, Michael C. (2010). Reflections on the development and contribution of critical systems thinking and practice. (Research Paper) (Report). *Systems Re search and Behavioral Science*, 27(2), 133.

44 Erratum to "Buy Now and Match Later: Impact of Posterior Price Matching on Profit with Strategic Consumers". (2010). *Manufacturing & Service Operations Management*, 12(2), 370.

45 Morin, E., & Kern, A. (1999). Homeland earth: *A manifesto for the new millennium* (Advances in systems theory, complexity, and the human sciences). Cresskill, N.J.: Hampton Press.

46 Hammond, D., & Merchant, Carolyn. (1997). *Toward a Science of Synthesis: The Heritage of General Systems Theory*, ProQuest Dissertations and Theses.

47 Hammond, et al., 1997.

48 Piaget, J. (2003). *The psychology of intelligence* (2nd ed., Routledge Classics). London: Routledge.

49 Senge, Peter M. (2000). Systems Change in Education. Reflections: *The SoL Journal*, 1(3), 52-60.

50 Weber, M. (2002). *The Protestant ethic and the spirit of capitalism* (3rd Roxbury ed.). Los Angeles, Calif.: Roxbury Pub.

51 Herzog, L. (2018). Durkheim on Social Justice: The Argument from "Organic Solidarity". *American Political Science Review*, 112(1), 112-124.

52 Shilling, C., & Mellor, P. (2011). Retheorising Emile Durkeim on Society and Religion: Embodiment, Intoxication and Collective Life. *The Sociological Review*, 59(1), 17-41.

DOUBT

Figure 5. Environment vs Consumer Input and Output
Figure 6. Estimating Current Extinction Rates
Figure 7. Prisoner's Dilemma Payoff Matrix

53 White, C., Carolina Biological Supply Company & Ca bisco Teleproductions. (1992). *Map of life science, society, and the Human Genome Project*. Burlington, N.C.: Carolina Biological Supply. (https://www.genome.gov/10001772/all-about-the--human-genome-project-hgp/).

54 Lewis, M. (2001). *Next: The Future Just Happened*. W.W. Norton & company.

55 Meeker, J. (1974). T*he comedy of survival; studies in literary ecology.* New York: Scribner.

56 Skyrms, B. (2001). The Stag Hunt. *Proceedings and Addresses of the American Philosophical Association*, 75(2), 31-41.

57 "Selfridge-Conway procedure," (https://en.wikipedia.org/wiki/Selfridge—Conway_procedure).

58 Roediger, H., & Desoto, K. (2016). Recognizing the
Presidents: Was Alexander Hamilton President?
Psychological Science, 27(5), 644-50.

59 Carter, B. (2015). Meacham, Jon: Thomas Jefferson:
President & Philosopher. *The Horn Book Guide*,
26(1), 195.

60 *President James Madison's First Inaugural Address*, 1809.
(n.d.). Great Neck Publishing.

61 Vorobsev, N. (1994). *Foundations of game theory:
Noncooperative games*. Basel; Boston: Birkheauser.

62 Rousseau, J. (1968). *The social contract* (The Penguin
classics; L201). Harmondsworth: Penguin.

63 Pothos, Perry, Coor, Matthew, & Busemeyer. (2011).
Understanding cooperation in the Prisoner's Dilemma
game. *Personality and individual Differences*, 51(3),
210-215.

64 Hardin, G. (1968). The tragedy of the commons. *Science*,
162(3859), 1243-1248.

65 Hobbes, T., & Missner, M. (2016). *Thomas Hobbes:
Leviathan* (Longman Library of Primary Sources).

66 Spinelli, M., Carvalho, R., Silva, H., Brandao, S., &
Frutuoso, M. (2016). Sustainable study of the an
thropic carrying capacity and its influence on the
point of equilibrium of the environmental resilience.
Revista Brasileira De Georgrafia Fisico, 9(1), 185-199.

67 Environmental Determinism? (2012). Science,
336(6087), 1358.

68 "Human-Environment Relations, M.S. (Ithaca),"
(https://gradschool.cornell.edu/academics/
fields-of-study/subject/design-and-environmental-
analysis/human-environment-relations-ms-ithaca).

69 "The Prisoner's Dilemma in detail,"
(http://www.open.edu/openlearn/history-the-arts/
culture/philosophy/the-prisoners-dilemma-detail).

70 Antin, Eleanor, Lacy, Suzanne, & Young, Gillian Turner.
(2014). Group Think. *PAJ: A Journal of Performance
and Art*, 36(2), 108-115.

Nature, the genome of diversity

Figure 8. Game 1, 2 Payoff Matrix

71 Richards, D. (2009). Economics and "Nature's Standard": Wes Jackson and The Land Institute. *Review of Radical Political Economics*, 41(2), 186-195.

72 Aligica, P. (2010). ELINOR OSTROM – NOBEL PRIZE IN ECONOMICS 2009. *Economic Affairs*, 30(1), 95-96.

73 Vriend, Nicolaas J. (2000). Demonstrating the Possibility of Pareto Inferior Nash Equilibria. *Journal of Economic Education*, 31(4), 358-62.

74 Ophuls, W. (1973). Leviathan or Oblivion. In Toward a Steady State Economy, ed. H. E. Daly, p. 228. San Francisco: Freeman.

75 Ibid, (1973), p. 229.

76 Hardin (1968), Tragedy of the Commons.

77 Ostrom, E. (1990), *Governing the commons*, p. 10.

78 Ibid, (1990), p. 10.

INDETERMINACY

Figure 9. Game 3 with Complete Information
Figure 10. Game 3 with Incomplete Information

79 Michael Graves. (1978). *Fargo-Moorhead Cultural Bridge, Project Fargo, North Dakota and Moorhead, Minnesota South Elevation*, Data from: The Museum of Modern Art.

80 Goldberger, P. (1979). "Delirious New York" by Rem Koolhaas (Book Review). *The New York Review of Books*, 26(10), 15.

81 Wines, Jodidio, & Jodidio, Philip. (2000). *Green architec ture*. Koln; New York: Taschen.

82 Shannon, C., & Weaver, W. (1998). *The mathematical theory of communication*. Urbana: University of Illinois Press.

83 Venturi, R., & Museum of Modern Art. (1966). *Complexity and contradiction in architecture. With an introduction by Vincent Scully.* (Museum of Modern Art (New York, N.Y.). Papers on architecture;1). New York: Museum of Modern Art; distributed by Double day, Garden City, N.Y.

84 "Venturi, MoMA," (https://www.moma.org/artists/6132).

85 Ostrom, (1990), p. 11.

86 Ibid, (1990), p. 12.

Generative and Fanciful

87 Cricks, J. (2016). Frederick The Great: King of Prussia. *Military Review*, 96(6), 138.

88 Bach, J., & Frederick II. (n.d.). *The musical offering = (Das musikalische Opfer).* Scarsdale, N.Y.: E.F. Kalmus Orchestra Scores.

89 Tallis, T., Phillips, P., & Tallis Scholars. (1985). *Spem in alium [the 40-part motet...].* Oxford, England: Gimell.

90 Cache, B. (2002). Gottfried Semper: Stereotomy, Biology, and Geometry. *Perspecta*, 33, 80- 87

.91 Lynn, Greg. (1998). Embryonic House (stereolithography model).

92 Sterman, J. (2006). Learning from evidence in a complex world. *American Journal of Public Health*, 96(3), 505-14.

SYNCHRONICITY

93 Eberhard, K. (2008). Gottfried Wilhelm Leibniz. 743-745.

94 "Gottfried Wilhelm Leibniz," (https://plato.stanford.edu/entries/leibniz/).

95 Kennedy, S. (2011). *The Klan unmasked.* Tuscaloosa, Ala.: University of Alabama Press.

96 Secrets and agents; Information asymmetry. (2016). The Economist, 420(8999), 55-56.

97 "Stetson Kennedy; Infiltrated Klu Klux Klan,"
    (http://www.nytimes.com/2011/08/29/us/
    29kennedy.html).

98 (https://www.youtube.com/watch?v=Xs0K4ApWl4g).

99 Levitt, S., & Dubner, S. (2006). Freakonomics: A rogue
    economist explores the hidden side of everything
    (Rev. and expanded ed.). New York, NY:
    William Morrow.

100 Carson, R. (1962). Silent spring. Boston: Houghton Mifflin.

101 "Rachel Carsons Critics Keep On But She Told Truth About
    DDT,"(https://e360.yale.edu/features/rachel_car
    sons_critics_keep_on_but_she_told_truth_about_
    ddt).

102 Gibney, Coyote, McLean, Elkind, Hauser, Gibney, Alex,...
    Magnolia Home Entertainment. (2006). *Enron the
    smartest guys in the room*. Los Angeles, CA: Magnolia
    Home Entertainment.

103 Kennedy, Marshall, Ross, Sindell, Maguire, Bridges,...
    MCA Inc. (2003). *Seabiscuit* (Full screen
    presentation.,ed.). Universal City, CA: Universal.

104 "Critical Practice in an Age of Complexity," (http://
    architecturemps.com/wp-content/uploads/2018/02/
    Darla_Lindberg_The-Twenty-Year-Lag-and-Why-It-
    Matters_Abstract-UoA.pdf.

105 "How Much Time Do Kids Spend With Technology,"
    (http://learningworksforkids.com/2015/07/how-
    much-time-do-kids-spend-with-technology/).

106 "Digital Native,"
    (https://www.techopedia.com/definition/28094/
    digital-native).

107 "American Dreams Are Powered By College Completion,"
    (https://completecollege.org).

108 "Trying to Conceive After 35? What are the Risks of Birth
    Defects?"(https://www.babyhopes.com/articles/
    birthdefects.html).

109 "Did You Know? Neo Age,"
(https://www.alvarezandmarsal.com/sites/default/
files/files/Age-CEO-CFO-COO.pdf).

110 "How old and experienced is an average CEO?"
(http://thecontextofthings.com/2014/08/25/age-and-
experience-of-average-ceo/).

112 Benner, S. (1904). *Benner's prophecies of future ups and
downs in prices: What years to make money on pig-
iron, hogs, corn, and provisions*. The R. Clarke company.

113 Benner, (1904).

114 "Elliott Wave Principle,"
(https://en.wikipedia.org/wiki/Elliott_wave_
principle).

115 Mitchell, T. (1997). *Machine Learning*. New York:
McGraw-Hill.

Moralist turned economist

116 De Botton, A. (1997). How Proust can change your life:
Not a novel (1st ed.). New York: Pantheon Books.

117 De Botton, (1997).

118 Smith, A. (2001). *An Inquiry into the nature and causes of
the wealth of nations.* London: Electric Book.

119 Everitt, B. (2002). Markov Chain. 234.

120 Certeau, M. (1988). *The writing of history* (European
perspectives). New York: Columbia University Press.

121 Kossuth, Robert. (2000). Boondoggling, Baseball, and the
WPA. (Work Progress/Projects Administration).
Nine, 56.

122 "Tribute to American Women,"
(https://www.nytimes.com/1945/06/23/archives/
let ters-to-the-times-tribute-to-american-women-en
glish-woman-thanks.html).

123 "Dating Habits: Shortage of Men in the 1940s," (https://
enlightenedwomen.org/dating-habits-shortage-of-
men-in-the-1940s).

124 Riquier, A. (2015, July 30). Worst Post-WWII Economic Expansion is Even Worse. Investor's Business Daily, p. *Investor's Business Daily*, July 30, 2015.

125 "History of the Gold Standard," (https://www.thebalance.com/what-is-the-history-of-the-gold-standard-3306136).

126 Alpanda, & Peralta-Alva. (2010). Oil crisis, energy-saving technological change and the stock market crash of 1973-74. *Review of Economic Dynamics*, 13(4), 824-842.

127 Mccown, J. (2002). Real interest rates in the early 1980s. *Applied Economics Letters*, 9(11), 739-743.

128 Sloan, Jon, & Balko, Radley. (2005). Who Killed PayPal? (Letters) (Letter to the Editor). *Reason,* 37(7), 9.

129 Ballhaus, Rebecca. (2014, October 10). Federal Election Commission allows new funding stream for political conventions. *The Wall Street Journal Eastern Edition*. The Wall Street Journal Eastern Edition, Oct 10, 2014, Vol.0(0).

130 Rushkoff, Douglas. (2005). The new alphabet. (civilization of gaming and interactive play) (Institute for Information Law and Policy Symposium: State of Play). New York Law School Law Review, 49(1), 45-49.

131 Paine, Begley, Horton, Nader, Sheen, Wadleigh,...Sony Pictures Home Entertainment. (2006). *Who killed the electric car?* Culver City, Calif.: Sony Pictures Home Entertainment.

132 Arthur, Paul. (2006). Wal-Mart: The High Cost of Low Price. (Movies That Mattered). *Film Comment*, 42(1), 41.

133 Brown, T. (2006). The Value of History to Public Health. *American Journal of Public Health*, 96(2), 208.

134 Ostrom, (1990), p. 15.

135 Fitzpatrick, J. (2012). *The fall and the ascent of man: How Genesis supports Darwin.*

136 "The Centre Pompidou celebrates its 40th anniversary!" (http://frenchculture.org/art-and- design/2693-cen tre-pompidou-40th-anniversary).

137 "The Prophetic Side of Archigram," (https://www.citylab.com/design/2017/11/the-pro phetic-side-of-archigram/545759).

138 "The Centre Pompidou," (http://frenchculture.org/art-and-design/2693-cen tre-pompidou-40th-anniversary).

139 Reyner Banham. (1996). Archigram. Grove Art Online, Grove Art Online.

140 Price, C., & Littlewood, J. (1968). The Fun Palace. The *Drama Review*: TDR, 12(3), 127-134.

141 "Renzo Piano and Richard Rogers' culture factory for the people: a building that at 40 year old, still looks to the future," (https://archpaper.com/2017/01/cen tre-pom pidou-turns-40).

142 Sara Miller Llana. (2017, January 22). The Pompidou at 40: How, despite terrorism, museum keeps Parisians coming. The Christian Science Monitor. *The Christian Science Monitor*, Jan 22, 2017.

143 "Renzo Piano and Richard Rogers' culture factory for the people,"(https://archpaper.com/2017/01/centre-pompidou-turns-40).

BIBLIOGRAPHY

"American Dreams Are Powered By College Completion," (https:// completecollege.org).

"Buckminster Fuller Institute," (https://www.bfi.org/).

"Critical Practice in an Age of Complexity," (http://architec turemps.com/wp-con-tent/uploads/2018/02/Dar la_Lindberg_The-Twenty-Year-Lag-and-Why-It-Matters_Abstract-UoA.pdf.

"Dating Habits: Shortage of Men in the 1940s," (https://en lightenedwomen.org/dating-habits-shortage-of-men -in-the-1940s).

"Did You Know? Neo Age," (https://www.alvarezandmarsal.com/sites/default/ files/files/Age-CEO-CFO-COO.pdf).

"Digital Native," (https://www.techopedia.com/definition/28094/ digital-native).

"Eighteenth Amendment to the Constitution," (https://en.wikipedia.org/wiki/Eighteenth_Amend ment_to_the_United_States_Constitution).

"Elliott Wave Principle," (https://en.wikipedia.org/wiki/Elliott_ wave_principle).

"Gottfried Wilhelm Leibniz," (https://plato.stanford.edu/ entries/leibniz/)."History of the Gold Standard," (https://www.thebalance.com/what-is-the-history-of -the-gold-standard-3306136).

"How Much Time Do Kids Spend With Technology," (http://learningworksforkids.com/2015/07/how-much-time-do-kids-spend-with-tech-nology/).

"How old and experienced is an average CEO?" (http://thecontextofthings.com/2014/08/25/ age-and-experience-of-average-ceo/).

"Human-Environment Relations, M.S. (Ithaca)," (https://gradschool.cornell.edu/academics/fields-of-study/subject/design-and-envi-ronmental-analysis/ human-environment-relations-ms-ithaca).

"Los Angeles Riots, 1992 (1)," (https://www.youtube.com/watch?v=P43W Zd611WA).

"Ludwig von Bertalanffy – General Systems Theory – 1950,"

"Orson Welles, War of the World," (https://www.youtube. com/watch?v=XsOK4ApWl4g).

"Renzo Piano and Richard Rogers' culture factory for the people: a building that at 40 year old, still looks to the future," (https://archpaper.com/2017/01/cen tre-pompidou-turns-40).

"Selfridge-Conway procedure," (https://en.wikipedia.org/ wiki/Selfridge–Conway_procedure).

"Stetson Kennedy; Infiltrated Klu Klux Klan," (http://www.ny times.com/2011/08/29/us/29kennedy.html).

"The California State University," (https://fresca.calstate.edu/ faculty/2545).

"The Centre Pompidou celebrates its 40th anniversary!" (http://frenchculture.org/art-and-design/2693-cen tre-pompidou-40th-anniversary).

"The Prisoner's Dilemma in detail," (http://www.open.edu/ openlearn/history-the-arts/culture/philosophy/ the-prisoners-dilemma-detail).

"The Prophetic Side of Archigram," (https://www.citylab.com/design/2017/11/the-pro phetic-side-of-archigram/545759).

"Tribute to American Women," (https://www.nytimes. com/1945/06/23/archives/letters-to-the-times-trib ute-to-american-women-english-woman-thanks. html).

"Trying to Conceive After 35? What are the Risks of Birth Defects?" (https://www.babyhopes.com/articles/ birthdefects.html).

"Rachel Carson's Critics Keep On But She Told Truth About DDT," (https://e360.yale.edu/features/rachel_car sons_critics_keep_on_but_she_told_truth_about_ ddt).

"Venturi, MoMA," (https://www.moma.org/artists/6132).

Ackoff, R. (1999). Re-creating the corporation a design of organizations for the 21st century. New York: Oxford University Press.

Aligica, P. (2010). ELINOR OSTROM – NOBEL PRIZE IN ECONOMICS 2009. Economic Affairs, 30(1), 95-96.

Alpanda, & Peralta-Alva. (2010). Oil crisis, energy-saving technological change and the stock market crash of 1973-74. Review of Economic Dynamics, 13(4), 824-842.

Antin, Eleanor, Lacy, Suzanne, & Young, Gillian Turner. (2014). Group Think. PAJ: A Journal of Performance and Art, 36(2), 108-115.

Arthur, Paul. (2006). Wal-Mart: The High Cost of Low Price. (Movies That Mattered). Film Comment, 42(1), 41.

Bach, J., & Frederick II. (n.d.). The musical offering = (Das musikalische Opfer). Scarsdale, N.Y.: E.F. Kalmus Orchestra Scores.

Bajcsy, R. (2010). Ubiquity symposium "What is computation?": Computation and infor-mation. Ubiquity,2010(December), Ubiquity, 01 December 2010, Vol.2010(December).

Ballhaus, Rebecca. (2014, October 10). Federal Election Com mission allows new funding stream for political conventions.The Wall Street Journal Eastern Edition. The Wall Street Journal Eastern Edition, Oct 10, 2014, Vol.0(0).

Banathy, B. (1996). Designing social systems in a changing world (Contemporary systems thinking). New York: Plenum Press.

Banathy, B., & Jenlink, P. (2005). Dialogue as a Means of Collective Communication.

Benner, S. (1904). Benner's prophecies of future ups and downs in prices: What years to make money on pig-iron, hogs, corn, and provisions. The R. Clarke company.

Bertalanffy, L. (1969). General system theory; foundations, development, applications. New York: George Braziller.

Darla V. Lindberg

Bertalanffy, L., & LaViolette, P. (1981). A systems view of man. Boulder, Colo.: Westview.

Boulding, K., Dolfsma, W., & Kesting, S. (2013). Interdisciplinary economics Kenneth E. Boulding's engagement in the sciences (Routledge Studies in the History of Economics). Abingdon [England]: Routledge.

Blum, M. (2016). Cybernetics: A mathematician of mind. Nature, 538(7623), 39-40.

Brown, T. (2006). The Value of History to Public Health. American Journal of Public Health, 96(2), 208.

Burke, E., & Ritchie, D. (1992). Further reflections on the revolution in France. Indianapolis: Liberty Fund.

Cache, B. (2002). Gottfried Semper: Stereotomy, Biology, and Geometry. Perspecta, 33, 80- 87.

Capra, F. (1982). The turning point: Science, society, and the rising culture. New York: Simon and Schuster.

Capra, F. (1996). The web of life: A new scientific understanding of living systems (1st Anchor Books ed.). New York: Anchor Books.

Carson, R. (1962). Silent spring. Boston: Houghton Mifflin.

Carter, B. (2015). Meacham, Jon: Thomas Jefferson: President & Philosopher. The Horn Book Guide, 26(1), 195.

Certeau, M. (1988). The writing of history (European perspectives). New York: Columbia University Press.

Chapanis, A. (1958). An Introduction to Cybernetics. W. Ross Ashby. The Quarterly Review of Biology, 33(1), 97.

Checkland, P. (1999). Systems thinking, systems practice (New ed.). Chichester, England; New York; John Wiley.

Cricks, J. (2016). Frederick The Great: King of Prussia. Military Review, 96(6), 138.

De Botton, A. (1997). How Proust can change your life: Not a novel (1st ed.). New York: Pan-theon Books.

Eberhard, K. (2008). Gottfried Wilhelm Leibniz. 743-745.
Elliott, C. (1992). Technics and architecture: The development of materials and systems for buildings. Cambridge, Mass.: MIT Press.

Environmental Determinism? (2012). Science, 336(6087), 1358.

Erratum to "Buy Now and Match Later: Impact of Posterior Price Matching on Profit with Strate-gic Consumers." (2010). Manufacturing & Service Operations Management, 12(2), 370.

Everitt, B. (2002). Markov Chain. 234.

Fitzpatrick, J. (2012). The fall and the ascent of man: How Genesis supports Darwin.

Flood, R. (2017). Thirty Years of Systemic Practice and Action Research. Systemic Practice and Action Research, 30(3), 209-211.

Fuller, R. (1983). Inventions (1st ed.). New York: St. Martin's Press. Gibney, Coyote, McLean, Elkind, Hauser, Gibney, Alex,...Magnolia Home Entertainment. (2006). Enron the smartest guys in the room. Los Angeles, CA: Magnolia Home Entertainment.

Gideon. (n.d.). Chadwyck-Healey.

Goldberger, P. (1979). "Delirious New York" by Rem Koolhaas (Book Review). The New York Review of Books, 26(10), 15.

Hammond, D., & Merchant, Carolyn. (1997). Toward a Science of Synthesis: The Heritage of General Systems Theory, ProQuest Dissertations and Theses.

Hardin, G. (1968). The tragedy of the commons. Science, 162(3859), 1243-1248. Herzog, L. (2018). Durkheim on Social Justice: The Argument from "Organic Solidarity". American Political Science Review, 112(1), 112-124.

Hobbes, T., & Missner, M. (2016). Thomas Hobbes: Leviathan (Longman Library of Primary Sources).

Jackson, Michael C. (2010). Reflections on the development
and contribution of critical systems thinking and
practice. (Research Paper) (Report). Systems
Research and Behavioral Science, 27(2), 133.

Kennedy, Marshall, Ross, Sindell, Maguire, Bridges,...MCA Inc.
(2003). Seabiscuit (Full screen presentation., ed.).
Universal City, CA: Universal.
Kennedy, S. (2011). The Klan unmasked. Tuscaloosa, Ala.:
University of Alabama Press.

Kossuth, Robert. (2000). Boondoggling, Baseball, and the
WPA. (Work Progress/Projects Administration). Nine,
56.

Leonard, A. (2015). Stafford Beer and the legacy of Cybersyn:
Seeing around corners. Kybernetes, 44(6/7), 926-934.

Levitt, S., & Dubner, S. (2006). Freakonomics: A rogue
economist explores the hidden side of everything
(Rev. and expanded ed.). New York, NY: William
Morrow.

Lewis, M. (2001). Next: The Future Just Happened.
W.W. Norton & company.

Luhmann, N., & Barrett, R. (2012). Theory of society Volume
1 (Cultural memory in the present). Stanford, Calif.:
Stanford University Press.

Lynn, Greg. (1998). Embryonic House (stereolithography
model).

Maturana, H., & Varela, F. (1980). Autopoiesis and cognition:
The realization of the living (Boston studies in the
philosophy of science; v. 42). Dordrecht, Holland;
Boston: D. Reidel Pub.

Mccown, J. (2002). Real interest rates in the early 1980s.
Applied Economics Letters, 9(11), 739-743.

Meeker, J. (1974). The comedy of survival; studies in literary
ecology. New York: Scribner.

Michael Graves. (1978). Fargo-Moorhead Cultural Bridge,
Project Fargo, North Dakota and Moorhead,
Minnesota South Elevation, Data from: The Museum
of Modern Art.

Mitchell, T. (1997). Machine Learning. New York: McGraw-Hill.

Morgan, & Morgan, Morris Hicky. (1960). Vitruvius: The ten books on architecture. New York: Dover Publications.

Morin, E., & Kern, A. (1999). Homeland earth: A manifesto for the new millennium. (Ad-vances in systems theory, complexity, and the human sciences). Cresskill, N.J.: Hamp-ton Press.

Napp, N., & Nagpal, R. (2014). Distributed amorphous ramp construction in unstructured environments. 32(2), 279-290.

Nechansky, H. (2010). The relationship between: Miller's living systems theory and Beer's viable systems theory. Systems Research and Behavioral Science, 27(1), 97-112.

Odum, E. (1993). Ecology and our endangered life-support systems (2nd ed.). Sunderland, Mass.: Sinauer Associates.

Odum, H. (2007). Environment, power, and society for the twenty-first century the hierarchy of energy (New ed.). New York; Chichester: Columbia University Press.

Ophuls, W. (1973). Leviathan or Oblivion. In Toward a Steady State Economy, ed. H. E. Daly, p. 228. San Francisco: Freeman.

Ostrom, E. (1990). Governing the commons: The evolution of institutions for collective action (Political econo my of institutions and decisions). Cambridge; New York: Cambridge University Press.

Paine, Begley, Horton, Nader, Sheen, Wadleigh,...Sony Pictures Home Entertainment. (2006). Who killed the electric car? Culver City, Calif.: Sony Pictures Home Entertainment.

Parsons, T. (1977). Social systems and the evolution of action theory. New York: Free Press.

Parsons, T. (1978). Action theory and the human condition. New York: Free Press. Parsons, T. (1969). Politics and social structure. New York: Free Press.

Piaget, J. (2003). The psychology of intelligence (2nd ed., Rout ledge Classics). London: Routledge.

Porter, Kak, Porter, William A, & Kak, Subhash. (1989).
　　　　Advances in communications and signal processing
　　　　(Lecture Notes in control and information
　　　　sciences;129). Berlin; New York: Springer-Verlag.

Pothos, Perry, Coor, Matthew, & Busemeyer. (2011). Under
　　　　standing cooperation in the Prisoner's Dilemma
　　　　game. Personality and individual Differences, 51(3),
　　　　210-215.
President James Madison's First Inaugural Address, 1809.
　　　　(n.d.). Great Neck Publishing.

Price, C., & Littlewood, J. (1968). The Fun Palace. The Drama
　　　　Review: TDR, 12(3), 127-134.

Prietula, Carley, Gasser, Prietula, Michael J, Carley, Kathleen
　　　　M, & Gasser, Leslie George. (1998). Simulating
　　　　organizations: Computational models of institutions
　　　　and groups. Menlo Park, CA: AAAI Press/MIT Press.

Prigogine, I. (1980). From being to becoming: Time and com
　　　　plexity in the physical sciences. San Francisco: W. H.
　　　　Freeman.

Reyner Banham. (1996). Archigram. Grove Art Online, Grove
　　　　Art Online.

Richards, D. (2009). Economics and "Nature's Standard": Wes
　　　　Jackson and The Land Institute. Review of Radical
　　　　Political Economics, 41(2), 186-195.

Riquier, A. (2015, July 30). Worst Post-WWII Economic Expan
　　　　sion is Even Worse. Investor's Business Daily,
　　　　p. Investor's Business Daily, July 30, 2015.

Roediger, H., & Desoto, K. (2016). Recognizing the Presidents:
　　　　Was Alexander Hamilton President? Psychological
　　　　Science, 27(5), 644-50.

Rousseau, J. (1968). The social contract (The Penguin classics;
　　　　L201). Harmondsworth: Penguin.

Rushkoff, Douglas. (2005). The new alphabet. (civilization of
　　　　gaming and interactive play) (Institute for
　　　　Information Law and Policy Symposium: State of
　　　　Play). New York Law School Law Review, 49(1), 45-49.

Sara Miller Llana. (2017, January 22). The Pompidou at 40: How, despite terrorism, museum keeps Parisians coming. The Christian Science Monitor. The Christian Science Monitor, Jan 22, 2017.

Saraiya, S. (2017). The 1992 L.A. Riots, a Quarter-Century Later. Variety, 335(14), 133.

Sarne, D., & Grosz, B. (2013). Determining the value of information for collaborative multi-agent planning. Autonomous Agents and Multi-Agent Systems, 26(3), 456-496.

Secrets and agents; Information asymmetry. (2016). The Economist, 420(8999), 55-56.

Senge, P. (1999). The Dance of change: The challenges of sustaining momentum in learning organizations (1st ed.). New York: Currency/Doubleday.

Senge, Peter M. (2000). Systems Change in Education. Reflections: The SoL Journal, 1(3), 52-60.

Shilling, C., & Mellor, P. (2011). Retheorising Emile Durkeim on Society and Religion: Embodiment, Intoxication and Collective Life. The Sociological Review, 59(1), 17-41.

Shannon, C., & Weaver, W. (1998). The mathematical theory of communication. Urbana: University of Illinois Press.

Skyrms, B. (2001). The Stag Hunt. Proceedings and Addresses of the American Philosophical Association, 75(2), 31- 41.

Sloan, Jon, & Balko, Radley. (2005). Who Killed PayPal? (Letters) (Letter to the Editor). Reason, 37(7), 9.

Smith, A. (2001). An Inquiry into the nature and causes of the wealth of nations. London: Electric Book.

Spinelli, M., Carvalho, R., Silva, H., Brandao, S., & Frutuoso, M. (2016).   Sustainable study of the anthropic carrying capacity and its influence on the point of equilibrium of the environmental resilience. Revista Brasileira De Georgrafia Fisico, 9(1), 185-199.

Sterman, J. (2006). Learning from evidence in a complex world. American Journal of Public Health, 96(3), 505-14.

Stichweh, R. (2000). Systems theory as an alternative to action theory?; the rise of 'communication' as a theoretical option. Acta Sociologica, 43, 5-13.

Swanson, R. (2010). Foundations of Human-resource Development (2nd ed.). Human Resource Management International Digest, 18(7), 142-144.

Tallis, T., Phillips, P., & Tallis Scholars. (1985). Spem in alium [the 40-part motet...]. Oxford, England: Gimell.

Twomey, J. (2004). SEARCHING FOR A LEGACY: THE LOS ANGELES TIMES, COLLECTIVE MEMORY AND THE 10TH ANNIVERSARY OF THE 1992 L.A. "RIOTS'. Race, Gender & Class, 11(1), 75.

Venturi, R., & Museum of Modern Art. (1966). Complexity and contradiction in architecture.With an introduction by Vincent Scully. (Museum of Modern Art (New York, N.Y.).Papers on architecture;1).New York: Museum of Modern Art; distributed by Doubleday,Garden City, N.Y.

Vorobsev, N. (1994). Foundations of game theory: Noncooperative games. Basel; Boston: Birkheauser.

Vriend, Nicolaas J. (2000). Demonstrating the Possibility of Pareto Inferior Nash Equilibria. Journal of Economic Education, 31(4), 358-62.

Weber, M. (2002). The Protestant ethic and the spirit of capitalism (3rd Roxbury ed.). Los Angeles, Calif.: Roxbury Pub.

White, C., Carolina Biological Supply Company & Cabisco Teleproductions. (1992). Map of life science, society, and the Human Genome Project. Burlington, N.C.: CarolinaBiological Supply.(https://www.genome.gov/10001772/all-about-the--human-genome-project-hgp/).

Wines, Jodidio, & Jodidio, Philip. (2000). Green architecture. Koln; New York: Taschen.